AF609403

THE Spooky Season HANDBOOK

BLOOMSBURY PUBLISHING
Bloomsbury Publishing Plc
50 Bedford Square, London, WC1B 3DP, UK
29 Earlsfort Terrace, Dublin 2, Ireland

BLOOMSBURY, BLOOMSBURY PUBLISHING and the Diana logo are trademarks of Bloomsbury Publishing Plc

First published in Great Britain 2025

Copyright © Bloomsbury Publishing Plc, 2025

Bloomsbury Publishing Plc is identified as the author of this work in accordance with the Copyright, Designs and Patents Act 1988.

All rights reserved. No part of this publication may be: i) reproduced or transmitted in any form, electronic or mechanical, including photocopying, recording or by means of any information storage or retrieval system without prior permission in writing from the publishers; or ii) used or reproduced in any way for the training, development or operation of artificial intelligence (AI) technologies, including generative AI technologies. The rights holders expressly reserve this publication from the text and data mining exception as per Article 4(3) of the Digital Single Market Directive (EU) 2019/790

Bloomsbury Publishing Plc does not have any control over, or responsibility for, any third-party websites referred to in this book. All internet addresses given in this book were correct at the time of going to press. The author and publisher regret any inconvenience caused if addresses have changed or sites have ceased to exist, but can accept no responsibility for any such changes

A catalogue record for this book is available from the British Library

Library of Congress Cataloguing-in-Publication data has been applied for

ISBN: HB: 978-1-5266-9751-6; eBook: 978-1-5266-9850-6

2 4 6 8 10 9 7 5 3 1

Commissioning editor: Samhita Foria
Designer and illustrator: George Saad
Production controller: Ben Chisnall

Printed and bound in Great Britain by CPI Group (UK) Ltd, Croydon CR0 4YY

To find out more about our authors and books visit www.bloomsbury.com and sign up for our newsletters

THE Spooky Season HANDBOOK

The ultimate guide to celebrating the best time of year

BEA WITCHED

BLOOMSBURY

CONTENTS

AN INTRODUCTORY ODE TO SPOOKY SEASON

When the air turns crisp at the very beginning of autumn, there's a sudden hum of magic in it, and it keeps on thriving. The smoke of burning wood curls through the sky and its scent clings to clothes like a spell. Crinkled leaves drift and twirl towards the ground as trees shake off their old coats and the year gone by. They crunch so deliciously as you walk over them, a symphony of crackles that kindly accompanies your chilly afternoon stroll. As the season unfurls, time seems to slow down and everything becomes more and more mysterious. The end of October brings a rustle of something darker. The days are shrinking down and dusk approaches faster, which means that we spend more time tucked away in the shadows. For some, this is a beautiful place to be, here in the gloom, because magic also resides here. This is the essence of spooky season, one crowned by Halloween, which endures to keep this ancient observance of death alive.

Halloween has shapeshifted over many centuries – transforming into a global celebration of the mystical and macabre. Today's spooky festivities have roots in the folk traditions and beliefs from Celtic-speaking countries, with some thought to have even older Pagan origins. The earliest ritual with a suggested lineage to modern-day Halloween can be traced back over 2,000 years to the Gaelic festival of Samhain (pronounced *sow-in*), celebrated on 31 October or 1 November in what is now known as Ireland, the United Kingdom and northern France. It marked the end of harvest season and the approach of frosty winter months, which at the time held associations with death, darkness and liminality. It is in this liminal space, between light and dark, that spooky season is born.

On the night of Samhain, the Celts believed that the veil between our mortal realm and the deceased became thinner, meaning that spirits could return to earth and even interact with the living. This included the 'Aos Sí', or fairy folk, a mischievous supernatural race that would set out to lure people back into their own otherworldly domain. These creatures were appeased by leaving out food and other gracious offerings outside your home. To avoid being recognised by wandering ghosts, particularly the vengeful ones, people would often wear disguises in the form of animal skins and costumes – a practice widely regarded as one of the earliest inspirations for costuming traditions during Halloween.

As Christianity expanded across the European continent, the Church sought to replace Pagan holidays with their own. In the seventh century, Pope Boniface IV established All Saints' Day, also known as All Hallows' Day, celebrated on 13 May in tribute to every saint. A century later, Pope Gregory III moved this celebration to 1 November, likely to coincide with Samhain and ease the shift for newly converted Christians. The evening before All Hallows' Day was known as All Hallows' Eve, which later became the name more recognisable to present-day revellers: Hallowe'en. Then came the English Reformation, led by the notorious King Henry VIII, which severed various ties to Catholic traditions in favour of the Church of England. Halloween lost much of its religious significance during this time, though it remained popular as a secular holiday.

With the turn of the twentieth century, Halloween underwent another metamorphosis into an increasingly jubilant and family-friendly holiday. Throughout the Roaring Twenties and Thirties, it took hold across the US, with lavish costume parties, trick-or-treating and parades becoming seasonal staples year after year. Following The Second World War, the baby boom continued to reshape the holiday into a children's celebration, bringing with it a hoard of mass-produced costumes and candy. Though Halloween is most prominent in the US, Canada and the UK, the mystical charm of the holiday has seeped its way into other corners of the globe. Places such as Japan, Brazil and other parts of Europe have woven these festivities, already cloaked in ancient lore, into their own cultural curiosities and traditions.

In this modern world, hyperconnected by wires and screens, our lives move at lightning-speed while slower traditions and observations of the natural world are left behind. We are so often starved of enchantment, mystery and whimsy that we forget to admire the gentle beauty of the sunrise or listen to the dawn chorus of singing birds. Autumn is a reminder to pause and reconnect with the world. It is the season for letting go and accepting the strange beauty of decay, just like the falling leaves that die so exquisitely in shades of amber, russet, plum and shining gold. During these months, it seems easier to recall just how primordial the earth is, as if the ancient rhythms of Mother Nature begin to stir a little louder. Now is the time to listen closely.

Spooky season, with its jubilant celebration of the magical and grotesque, can help us return to a more spiritual relationship with nature, ourselves and our loved ones. Halloween calls us to embrace our morbid curiosities while honouring those who have passed on. It encourages us to revel in the whimsical joy of dressing up while remembering who we truly are beneath the costume. It makes us a little braver and wilder, possessed by the spirit of transformation that autumn and Halloween mirror so profoundly.

This book is for those who long to sink their hands into the earth's soil, whisper folktales so they are not forgotten or howl secrets at the moon. Within these pages, you'll find recipes to warm your belly and rituals to soothe your soul. There are crafts and quiet meditations to guide you in honouring the season with purpose, reverence and a little mischief. Discover curated films, books and playlists that let you sink your teeth into the eerie atmosphere.

Here, you are welcomed to embrace both the trick and the treat within you – for one cannot exist without the other. Those who cherish spooky season know this best of all.

Part 01

GETTING INTO THE SPIRIT

The truth is, if you adore Halloween, the last few lingering, lazy days of summer are likely spent waiting in anticipation for the best season of the year to arrive: the spooky kind, of course. Once you feel that first brush of crisp autumn air against your cheek, whispering the murmur of spellwork, you finally breathe a sigh of relief.

But even before that moment comes, and certainly after it does, there is no better feeling than truly getting into the spirit of it all. A frothy sip of Pumpkin Spice Latte (page 52). Watching that scary movie you've been dying to see (probably through your fingers). Reaching the end of a wickedly dark novel on a cosy October night. In this chapter, you'll find lovingly brewed recommendations, reflections and recipes for conjuring up the most mystical of moods.

Spooky season is upon us...

MOVIE WATCHLISTS FOR EVERY MOOD

Movies are magic – flickering images that dance across a screen and whisk you away to different realities. This season wouldn't be complete without a spooky movie marathon – or five. From blood-splattered slashers to more family-friendly frights, these watchlists have every festive feeling covered.

Don't forget to rustle up some seasonal snacks, such as Bloody Popcorn, page 151, or a punchy cocktail like a Poison Apple Cider, page 145, to steel your nerves.

* SPOOKY CLASSICS *

These tried-and-true horror films are classics for a reason, guaranteed to bring some ghoulishness to your movie night, along with a glint of old school charm. Returning to these timeless horrors again and again is the perfect way to pay homage to the spirit of the season, like consulting revered ancient texts.

1. A Nightmare on Elm Street (1984, Wes Craven)

A razor-gloved killer terrorises suburban teenagers while they sleep… from within their dreams. And it gets worse: if you die in your dreams, you die for real. This film introduced the world to the now iconic horror movie villain, Freddy Krueger, who delivers slasher suspense with a touch of the surreal and silly. The film centres on Nancy Thompson, a refreshingly brave and resourceful female protagonist, who must uncover her community's secret in order to survive Krueger's vengeful plans. *A Nightmare on Elm Street* is the perfect eighties horror: full of big hair and big kills. After watching, you might even think twice before drifting off to sleep.

2. The Haunting (1963, Robert Wise)

The haunted house is a winning trope in horror – creaking staircases, a sudden frigid draught, wandering mirror reflections. It's a crowd favourite! This film, based on Shirley Jackson's 1959 novel, *The Haunting of Hill House*, masterfully brings her classic story of ghostly disturbances to life (and death). A group of people are invited to the infamous Hill House to investigate some strange happenings taking place within its walls. No jumpscares or gore to be found here, only slow, creeping dread that grows spookier and spookier with each passing minute. Shot in stark black and white, *The Haunting* is also eerily beautiful. A more subtle scare that lingers nonetheless.

3. Suspiria (1977, Dario Argento)

Directed by the Italian horror maestro, Dario Argento, this surreal and stylistic masterpiece is a feral feast for the eyes. With vivid reds and blues splattered throughout its Gothic architectural setting, each frame is like a painting that hums with glamour and dread. The film follows Suzy Bannion, an American ballerina who travels to rural Germany to attend a prestigious dance academy, only to discover that a wicked secret is harboured there. This occultish movie will hypnotise you with its bright and beautiful aesthetics, but also leave you satisfyingly unsettled. *Suspiria* is truly executed in style.

4. Nosferatu: A Symphony of Horror (1922, F. W. Murnau)

This silent vampire film is a must-watch for any horror fan. An unauthorised adaptation of Bram Stoker's *Dracula*, its atmospheric and shadowy expressionism continues to inspire movie aesthetics to this day, over one hundred years later. Real estate agent Thomas Hutter travels from a fictional German town to the mountainous lands of Transylvania to meet with the mysterious Count Orlok, who just so happens to be a vampire, only to fall victim to his devilish plans to claim Thomas' young wife as his own. The bloodsucking Count, with his imposing height, clawed spindly fingers and pointed teeth, is pure monstrosity.

5. Psycho (1960, Alfred Hitchcock)

No homage to classics is complete without mention of Hitchcock, master of the psychological thriller. *Psycho* is a twisted tale of murder and mummy issues – a certified

Freudian nightmare. Who is predator and who is prey? This film will have you guessing at each new scene or shocking plot twist. A chilling look at the darker potentials of our human mind that is expertly crafted beginning to end. The shower sequence alone is one of the single greatest moments in cinema history. Get ready to check in to the Bates Motel… but beware, something salacious and sinister lurks nearby.

* BLOOD, GUTS, GORE! *

You've been warned: these next few are **not** for the faint of heart. From buckets of blood to nerve-shredding body horror, this is no place for the squeamish or weak-stomached.

If you dare take a peek, welcome! Let's see if you're brave enough to watch at least one of these films all the way through, a fearless commitment to celebrating Halloween in all its gory glory.

1. Dead Alive (1992, Peter Jackson)

Before *The Lord of the Rings* trilogy, director Peter Jackson made this zombie bloodbath. *Dead Alive*, also known as *Braindead*, is an outrageously gory addition to the undead subgenre. Set in 1950s New Zealand, this comedy horror centres on a timid young man, Lionel, who must deal with his overbearing mother, Vera, after she is turned into a zombie. With blood, blood and more blood, as well as marvellously creative practical effects, what follows is a carnival ride that is both side-splittingly funny and gross. This cult favourite is certainly not for the easily nauseated, but it does offer plenty of comic relief to counteract those grisly kills.

2. The Substance (2024, Coralie Fargeat)

This is a bold and bloody fairytale, and a cutting critique of the absurd beauty standards imposed on women. Set in Los Angeles, the film follows an ageing television star who gets her hands on a mysterious drug known as 'The Substance', which splits you into two versions of yourself – one being younger, successful and more stereotypically 'beautiful'. Unsurprisingly, this comes at a horrifying cost. Between its kitschy eighties aesthetics, scathing satirical bite and stomach-churning gore, this film is disturbingly entertaining. A full-on assault on our obsession with beauty: you just might be in the line of fire.

3. Hellraiser (1987, Clive Barker)

This darkly delicious film is one hell of a fever dream. A strange puzzle box opens a portal to another dimension filled with sadomasochistic creatures known as the Cenobites, who are consumed by sensation: pain and pleasure cannot be differentiated and so must be felt to their utmost extremes. Following this intriguing premise, *Hellraiser* is at its core an existential horror, but still provides more than enough gore, wrapped up in themes of desire and morality. It's worth seeing if only for the beautifully nightmarish makeup and special effects. But you'll also be rewarded with a thought-provoking watch that sticks with you long after the credits roll.

4. Inside (2007, Alexandre Bustillo and Julien Maury)

Originally titled *À l'intérieur*, this French horror follows Sarah, a heavily pregnant woman also in the process of grieving her partner, who is stalked back to her home on Christmas Eve by a mysterious woman who wants her unborn baby, and will stop at nothing to get it. Evoking the most primal depths of terror, you are confronted with an onslaught of violence that tests your nerves again and again. *Inside* is relentless, but it's also an unforgettably engrossing exploration of grief, motherhood and the urge to survive.

5. Evil Dead (2013, Fede Álvarez)

A reboot of the *Evil Dead* franchise, which began with the 1981 classic film by Sam Raimi, this instalment shocked viewers with its particularly gruesome approach. We join a group of five friends as they travel to a secluded cabin in the woods (this can't be good) to support Mia, who is battling drug addiction. As they attempt to guide her through this challenging time, they come across a strange ancient book, known as the Necronomicon, bound in human skin. Ignoring the *very* obvious warning signs, one of the friends begins to read from the ominous text (there's always one), unintentionally summoning a host of demonic forces that begin to possess the group one by one.

* CAMPY & COMICAL *

1. The Rocky Horror Picture Show (1975, Jim Sharman)

This is perhaps *the* archetypal Halloween movie. A beloved campy cult classic! This weird, wonderful and twisted musical brings the spirit of the season to life. *The Rocky Horror Picture Show* follows Brad and Janet, a newly married couple who become stranded during a storm and must seek shelter at a nearby mansion. They encounter a gang of eccentric characters, led by the fabulously freaky Dr Frank-N-Furter, a mad scientist from another planet who is fashioning his own Frankenstein-esque 'perfect man' called Rocky. The evening descends into glittery chaos – complete with fabulous musical performances and costumes. N.B. singing along is mandatory.

2. Scream (1996, Wes Craven)

This tongue-in-cheek satire of horror films is an essential watch for any seasoned fan of the genre, but don't expect it to follow the rules. As the movie twists and turns familiar tropes on their head, you won't know what's coming next. *Scream* is about a group of high school students in the small town of Woodsboro, where a masked killer, known as Ghostface, starts brutally murdering teenagers with a knife. The remaining survivors must solve the mystery of the killer's identity while avoiding the same fate. Though the film certainly has a grisly impact, its self-aware humour, laced with that classic nineties irony, is irresistibly droll.

3. Elvira: Mistress of the Dark (1988, James Signorelli)

The iconic Elvira, a hostess of horror TV, is a dark and sultry diva, sharp-tongued and never without her glamorous bouffant hairdo. In this film, she travels to a small town in New England after inheriting an old house there. Whether reckoning with conservative townsfolk or ancient familial curses, Elvira does everything in style and with a splash of humour. What better way to spend a spooky movie night than with this vampy goddess? Filled with saucy one-liners and lots of mystical mayhem, this horror-comedy just might be your new favourite to return to each year.

4. Ginger Snaps (2000, John Fawcett)

Hormonal, insatiable and full of rage: becoming a werewolf seems pretty close to the everyday experiences of a teenage girl. In *Ginger Snaps*, this parallel is made crystal clear. The film follows two outcast sisters, Ginger and Brigitte, in their small suburban town. When Ginger is bitten by a werewolf, the two must grapple with her transformation into a bloodthirsty and (even more) temperamental creature. As were-Ginger becomes increasingly violent, Brigitte must find a way to break the curse and save her sister. Packed with sardonic edge, this supernatural horror is both morbidly funny and a surprisingly poignant look at adolescence, puberty and budding desire.

5. Death Becomes Her (1992, Robert Zemeckis)

If *The Substance* seemed far too extreme for your tastes, this is the perfect substitute. Meryl Streep and Goldie

Hawn play rivals in this over-the-top campy farce. Both obsessed with staying young, the women consume a strange elixir that promises eternal youth to whoever drinks it, but they should have checked the fine print – for their bodies continue to decay while their spirits live on and on. What follows is a battle of the belles as these acting legends face off while trying to preserve their vanity. *Death Becomes Her* casts a spotlight on societal fears of women's ageing bodies, and the result is fabulously twisted.

✱ TO GET UNDER YOUR SKIN ✱

1. Hereditary (2018, Ari Aster)

Hereditary is a family horror-drama that revolves around the Grahams as they grieve the loss of their matriarch, Ellen. When they begin to uncover disturbing secrets about her past, supernatural terror descends on each family member as dark forces appear to be at play within their bloodline. Utterly chilling, this psychological trip will grasp you tight and not let go. A deeply unsettling but masterfully crafted horror story that slowly reveals the infected roots of an outwardly ordinary family tree.

2. We're All Going to The World's Fair (2021, Jane Schoenbrun)

An unnerving exploration of isolation and the dark side of the digital age, *We're All Going to The World's Fair* is an underrated gem. The film follows Casey, a lonely teenager who becomes obsessed with an online horror challenge known as the 'World's Fair' game. As she immerses herself into the experience, reality and fiction begin to blur, and she sinks further into the surreal liminal space it summons from within her attic bedroom. The tension in this strange and atmospheric movie builds subtly, crawling towards its disturbing climax. Absolutely worth a watch.

3. Don't Look Now (1973, Nicolas Roeg)

This haunting masterpiece, an adaptation of the 1971 short story by Daphne du Maurier of the same name, will drag you down, deeper and deeper, into its psychological depths. Set in Venice, it follows John and Laura Baxter, a grieving English couple who have lost their young daughter in a recent accident. While in the Italian city, John begins to experience unusual and disquieting events that appear almost supernatural in nature. As these eerie occurrences continue to unfold, his own grip on reality becomes weaker. This slow-burn horror is a powerful depiction of grief that doesn't hold back from the unsettling emotions that feed it.

4. The Wailing (2016, Na Hong-jin)

Taking place in a rural village in South Korea, this film blends elements of folklore, superstition and contemporary horrors. It centres on police officer Jong-Goo, who is called to investigate a series of mysterious illnesses and deaths that began with the arrival of a Japanese stranger to the village. Jong-Goo must identify who, or what, is behind these violent occurrences, with each step closer bringing more and more disturbing revelations. This unflinching story on the nature of evil, set against a foggy mountain range in the isolated countryside, will chill you to the bone.

5. Us (2019, Jordan Peele)

A mind-bending experience, *Us* delivers harrowing social commentary and darkly funny moments that are bound to stick with you. The film follows Adelaide Wilson and her family as they escape to their lakeside home for a getaway. This relaxing break is interrupted by the violent arrival of their all-too-real doppelgängers, who have plans to terrorise their more privileged life. As Adelaide and her family fight to survive, they must also confront the mysteries of their doubled existence. With each detail passionately crafted by Peele, from colour palettes to song choices, this film will have you turning your brain inside out so that you don't miss a single hidden meaning.

* FOR THE SCAREDY CATS *

A selection of films for you sensitive souls, who prefer a Halloween evening that is more cosy than nightmarish. These films bring a touch of eerie atmosphere without the guts and gore. Best enjoyed by flickering candlelight as you sip cinnamon tea under a fluffy blanket (don't worry, you won't need to hide underneath it).

1. Practical Magic (1998, Griffin Dunne)

This film perfectly blends autumnal warmth with a witchy edge. Set in a sleepy seaside town, it follows the Owens sisters, Sally (Sandra Bullock) and Gillian (Nicole Kidman), who were born into a long line of witches. Haunted by a centuries-old curse that states that any man who falls in love with an Owens woman will die, they must navigate love and loss with the help of one another and spellwork. A mystical, funny, sometimes bittersweet story about the triumphs of sisterly bonds, *Practical Magic* will have you dancing around the kitchen at midnight with a margarita in hand, enjoying the moon's glow.

2. Arsenic and Old Lace (1944, Frank Capra)

A screwball comedy that delivers Old Hollywood glamour with a thrilling twist. Mortimer Brewster (Cary Grant), a theatre critic and bachelor who has previously sworn off matrimony, finds himself newly married. Returning home to share this joyful news with the family, he instead discovers that his two sweet aunts, Abby and Martha, have a somewhat unusual pastime – poisoning lonely old men and burying them in the basement. A delicious satire of the American upper class that is equal parts funny and sharp, *Arsenic and Old Lace* is a forgotten classic about the skeletons we find in our family's closet.

3. Corpse Bride (2005, Tim Burton and Mike Johnson)

This beautifully crafted gothic fairytale is brought to life with spellbinding stop-motion. Set in a magically macabre Victorian world, it tells the story of Victor, a shy young man who accidentally proposes to Emily, a very sweet but nevertheless deceased bride-to-be, while practising his wedding vows (to a very much alive woman) in the woods. With this newly made marital oath, he is whisked away to the Land of the Dead. What follows is a film bursting with life, with jazz-playing skeletons, spider companions and a surprisingly tender-hearted love story. *Corpse Bride* is both spooky and romantic, one for the true yearners.

4. What We Do in the Shadows (2014, Taika Waititi and Jemaine Clement)

A mockumentary that poses the important question: how would the undead take to modern life? This cult comedy reimagines the formidable figure of the vampire in a more mundane setting. Taking place in the suburbs of Wellington, New Zealand, the film follows four vampire flatmates, Viago, Vladislav, Deacon and Petyr, as they bicker over chores, navigate their social lives and attempt to keep their bloodthirsty tendencies hidden from the humans around them. While absurd, *What We Do in the Shadows* is also a love letter to vampire lore. Its dry humour and surprisingly heartfelt moments are a beginner-friendly foray into a genre mostly marked by terror.

5. Kiki's Delivery Service (1989, Hayao Miyazaki)

This anime is an enchanting tale of growing up, finding independence and the everyday magic that surrounds us, brought to life by the legendary Studio Ghibli. It follows Kiki, a thirteen-year-old witch-in-training, as she leaves home to discover her purpose. With only a broomstick and her sarcastic cat, Jiji, she arrives in a bustling coastal city only to discover that starting over isn't easy. She opens a delivery service, flying around on her broom, interweaving herself with the community and slowly but surely learning what it means to be both a witch and herself. Set against a world filled with pastel hues and foggy bakery windows, *Kiki's Delivery Service* is a gentle yet affirming coming-of-age story.

5 HEX-CELLENT HALLOWEEN TV SPECIALS

Whether you're looking to return to a forgotten favourite, discover a new annual tradition or simply get your seasonal fix fast, these episodes serve up just the right amount of spook with a warm and fuzzy cosiness – perfect for crisp evenings bundled in blankets.

1. Charlie Brown, 'It's the Great Pumpkin' (1966)

Based on the *Peanuts* comic strip by legendary cartoonist Charles Schulz, this episode brings the toasty glow of nostalgia to spooky season. It follows the adventures of Charlie Brown and his friends during Halloween celebrations. His best friend, Linus, is waiting for the Great Pumpkin: a seasonal legend who emerges from a big pumpkin patch to deliver toys to well-behaved children. With some gentle spookiness and plenty of sweet and magical moments, this episode is whimsy come to life (plus, you're serenaded by a soothing jazz soundtrack).

2. Buffy the Vampire Slayer, 'Halloween' (1997 - Season 2, Episode 6)

Horror, humour, killer outfits – any *Buffy* episode makes for a rewarding Halloween watch, but this one takes place on the fateful night itself. When a mysterious new costume shop opens in Sunnydale, chaos ensues. Anyone wearing a costume from this store on Halloween night transforms into what they're dressed as. The kick-ass Buffy becomes a helpless eighteenth-century noblewoman, while her best friends, Xander and Willow, turn into a real soldier and invisible ghost. It's clever and creepy with plenty of nineties angst.

3. The Simpsons, 'Treehouse of Horror V' (1994 - Season 6, Episode 6)

These Halloween specials of the iconic animated show each contain three 'minisodes'. This fifth edition includes a brilliant spoof of Stanley Kubrick's *The Shining,* a metaphysical mind-melt when a broken toaster becomes a time machine, and some cannibalistic lunch ladies. It's absurd and often delightfully dark, as well as loaded with visual references that horror fans will love to spot. In a hurry? The 'Treehouse of Horror' is a satisfyingly speedy watch – three spooky stories in under half an hour.

4. Bewitched, 'Twitch or Treat' (1966 - Season 3, Episode 7)

What happens when a young witch tries to blend in as a typical suburban housewife? You get Samantha Stephens, along with some meddling family members and a whole lot of vintage charm. In this episode, Samantha's mother, also a witch, conjures up a new house to host a spectacular Halloween party, which ends up spiralling into classic sitcom mayhem. It's both campy and cute, ideal for those who crave something whimsical with a generous sprinkling of the supernatural.

5. Modern Family, 'Halloween' (2010 – Season 2, Episode 6)

Hilarity ensues when the dysfunctional yet loveable extended brood of *Modern Family* make plans to celebrate the holiday. The Dunphys, Pritchetts and Tucker-Pritchetts all get sucked into the spooky fun to varying results: costume mishaps, pranks gone-wrong and a haywire haunted house. Each character adds to the comedy, whether competitive or reluctant, a reminder that even the most frightful night of the year can be charmingly chaotic with your family.

10 BOOKS TO CURL UP WITH NEXT TO A CRACKLING FIRE

When autumn's breath becomes just a touch too bitterly cold, you can also embrace the seasonal spirit by curling up with a good book next to a warming fire or buried underneath your duvet. From spine-tingling reads to charmingly cosy delights, this selection of books will surely light your jack-o'-lantern. With each turn of the page, let the season envelop you like a forest fog.

1. Interview with the Vampire (1976, Anne Rice)

Anne Rice – queen of the undead. Beginning her legendary *Vampire Chronicles* series with this bloodthirsty classic, Rice redefined the genre with a decadent and decaying world of centuries-old vampires. Set in historic New Orleans, this first novel centres on the brooding vampire Louis, who recounts tales of his immortal existence to a curious reporter, including a complicated relationship with the charming but ruthless Lestat, another vampire. For those seduced by the dangers of supernatural beings, this gothic romance will satiate your desires.

2. The Leviathan (2022, Rosie Andrews)

Set in seventeenth-century Norfolk during the English Civil War, this historical novel is an enthralling tale of confronting forces beyond our understanding. A young soldier, Thomas Treadwater, is called home by his sister to investigate the sinister happenings brought on by the arrival of a new servant, Chrissa, who is facing charges of witchcraft. The rational Thomas must now come to terms with the superstitions that plague his family, and which might be all too real, connected to a shipwreck he survived years prior.

3. The Dangers of Smoking in Bed (2009, Mariana Enríquez)

A bone-chilling collection of short stories set in the gritty urban landscape of Argentina. Splicing folklore and contemporary social realities, these tales highlight the horrors of daily life through supernatural storytelling. Prepare to be unsettled from one story to the next as Enríquez delves deeper in the shadowy depths of the modern condition. *The Dangers of Smoking in Bed* is a ferocious feat – a reading experience that will gnaw at your mind even after you finish the last page.

4. Emily Wilde's Encyclopaedia of Faeries (2023, Heather Fawcett)

Your idea of pocket-sized and sweet fairies is probably *very* different from the rather vicious creatures that haunt European legends. This fantasy novel is a charming patchwork quilt of dark magic, Scandinavian folklore and a touch of romance. It follows Emily Wilde, a brilliant but socially awkward professor of faerie studies, as she travels to the rural village of Hrafnsvik, inspired by Iceland, in search of an elusive fae species known as the Hidden Ones. With her loyal dog, Shadow, in tow, as well as the flirtatious yet infuriating Wendell Bambleby, her professional rival, Emily is immersed into the secrets of the fae. *Emily Wilde's Encyclopaedia of Faeries* is cosy and whimsical, with a hint of the macabre.

5. The Bloody Chamber and Other Stories (1979, Angela Carter)

Your most beloved fairy tales – reimagined. This collection of short stories draws from the likes of *Bluebeard* and *Little Red Riding Hood*, transforming this familiar terrain into something chilling, carnal and uncanny. Allow yourself to be enticed by each fantastical realm, part-dream, part-nightmare, and revel in their strangely beautiful explorations of power, sexuality and myth. *The Bloody Chamber and Other Stories* evokes the energy of a shining full moon: alluring yet eerie, with a feminine bite.

6. The Silent Companions (2017, Laura Purcell)

This dark and atmospheric work of historical fiction is set against the backdrop of Victorian England. It follows the young Elsie, who is widowed and pregnant, as she seeks comfort in the old and unwelcoming country estate of her late husband. With those around her either resentful or unkind, she seeks companionship in the form of a painted wooden figure that looks uncannily like her, discovered behind a locked door. While others fear this strange object, Elsie pays no mind – until menacing events start to unfold.

7. Frankenstein (1818, Mary Shelley)

Who is more monstrous: the monster or its creator? Shelley posed this unsettling question when she was only eighteen years old. This Gothic classic follows Victor Frankenstein, a young scientist absorbed with discovering the secrets of mortality and death. His creation is a creature/man, spawned by unnatural means, who is rejected by society because of his perceived difference. Coaxed along by Shelley's hauntingly gorgeous prose, this story is one of deep philosophical complexity, unravelling the subtle horrors of existence and the prejudices we all carry.

8. Feast While You Can (2024, Mikaella Clements and Onjuli Datta)

Living in a small conservative town, Angelina Sicco must navigate her queerness within the isolation of this community. There also happens to be a ravenous monster living deep within a nearby mountain cave eyeing her up for its next meal. *Feast While You Can* interweaves ancient folklore and the modern hunt for a sense of belonging with stunning lyricism. Haunting and seductive, this horror romance will sink its razor-sharp teeth into you, and you won't want it to let go.

9. White is for Witching (2009, Helen Oyeyemi)

A novel steeped in gothic dread and magical realism. This delicately woven story of identity and familial bonds explores all the different kinds of ghosts that haunt us. *White is for Witching* follows Miranda Silver, a young woman with pica – a compulsion to eat inedible things such as plastic or chalk

– grappling with the recent death of her mother. When she moves away with the rest of the Silver family, the uncanny new house they inhabit appears to have a life of its own. Reading this bewitching novel is like shivers slowly inching their way up your spine.

10. Your Guide to Not Getting Murdered in a Quaint English Village

(2024, Maureen Johnson) Not only a murder mystery, but also a handy guidebook. Taking place in a picturesque English village that is not quite as idyllic as it seems, this cosy read pokes fun at the genre in a way that's both cunning and amusing. Be sure to pay attention: the author provides some sage advice on how to avoid a strange and suspicious death on your next visit to a quaint little village. After all, it's right there in the title.

GHOST STORIES TO WHISPER AFTER DARK

Telling ghost stories on Halloween night has long been part of its tradition, a harking back to its Samhain roots. But these stories have also been told across cultures and centuries, revealing the deep-rooted fears that cling to the people who tell them. These were often cautionary tales, passed down from generation to generation, to keep communities safe and make sense of the mysteries of life, death and everything in between. No matter where each story originates from, they're all eerily similar, for fear of the unknown transcends any one place, but also have one very particular thing in common – a woman is almost always at their centre.

More than that, these are often stories of vengeful women who were betrayed, silenced or mistreated, made monstrous through the terrifying tales told again and again due to fear of their stifled power suddenly being unleashed. So as you read these tales, and meet the spectral ladies that haunt them, take a moment to remember the many women throughout history that were victims of these patriarchal narratives.

La Llorona

The woman in white is a common ghostly figure that appears in many cultures, including La Llorona, usually translated as 'The Weeping Woman', who haunts Mexican folklore and tales from across Latin America. Myriad influences have shaped La Llorona's evolution, from pre-Columbian Aztec lore to European myths, following Spanish and Portuguese colonial rule. All these stories depict a grief-stricken woman who takes her own life after drowning her children in the river. The reason why depends on the version told, but it is usually out of jealousy, madness or anguish because of an unfaithful or abusive husband. She is then caught stuck in our earthly plane, wandering along riversides, by lakes and sometimes at crossroads in search of her slain kin. Her cries of despair can be heard in the dead of night, and encountering this apparition of a woman in white may result in death. La Llorona is more than mere ghost story, she is the very embodiment of torment, condemned to meander between worlds and forever bear the weight of a mother's unforgivable act.

Churels

The Churel of South and Southeast Asian folklore is a mythical creature born from the anguished spirit of a woman who dies unnaturally, while pregnant, in childbirth or from mistreatment at the hands of male family members. When a woman dies a traumatic or tragic death, her family may perform special rituals to prevent her spirit from returning as a Churel. This includes binding the body, burying her face down or reciting sacred texts to trap the spirit. While sometimes known to haunt lonely individuals and pregnant women, the Churel most often seeks revenge on the male figures who wronged her. She may appear as beautiful and enticing, seducing victims to lure them away from safety before revealing a black tongue, claw-like hands, sharp fangs and feet twisted backwards. The victim's life-force is then drained until they become shrivelled and aged or, in some versions, all of their blood is sucked from them. The Churel's unforgiving wrath, born from profound injustice, is a warning to those who abuse young women or simply fail to protect them.

THE HUMBLE PUMPKIN

With its rich orange hue and sweet earthy aroma, the humble pumpkin is the faithful companion of autumn. Native to the Americas, with earliest evidence dating the first pumpkin species back to between 7000 and 5500 BCE in what is now known as Mexico, the colourful squash was cultivated for thousands of years to become what it is today.

From about the fifteenth century, they made their way around the world along trade routes and were brought back to Europe by colonial settlers. There, pumpkins became not only a hearty food source, but also a symbol which is deeply intertwined with ritual and tradition.

In European folklore, the plump and round shape of pumpkins came to symbolise abundance, an emblem of harvest and seasonal changes. Through the affiliation between pumpkins and the ancient Celtic festival of Samhain, during which people carved faces into root vegetables to ward off evil spirits, they were also powerful sources of protection.

From their role as glowing guardians on our doorstep to the many nutritional benefits packed within their orange flesh, pumpkins truly are a devilish delight.

5 NO-WASTE WAYS TO DECORATE A PUMPKIN

Your Halloween pumpkins can live on beyond the 31st, whether baked into a sweet treat or served on the dinner table. These ideas are a wonderful way to take part in the rituals of the season without the waste! With a little bit of decorative sorcery, your pumpkins can still get a festive face-lift while remaining safe to eat (as soon as they're done bewitching your house guests and neighbours).

1. Haunted Hues

Your pumpkin can still shine bright on the front porch without the glow of a tealight. By making natural paints with ingredients you probably already have in your pantry, you can keep your pumpkin edible and compost friendly. Mix one tablespoon of water with about a teaspoon of turmeric, cocoa powder, some ground freeze-dried fruits or even activated charcoal to create a variety of colours. For a thicker consistency, mix in a teaspoon of cornstarch. Another option is to use edible cake pens, which come in a variety of colours and make crafting finer detail a little easier. With a paintbrush, fingertip or pen, get creative with spooky faces and shapes. You can also use carving stencils to draw on a perfectly haunted pumpkin.

2. Seasonal Garlands

On your next amble through the woods, search for leaves, twigs, flowers and any other foliage that catches your eye. When your seasonal stash is collected, attach these foraged items to some string or twine by creating tiny holes to pass the twine through, tying small knots to affix your woodland wonders in place. For added natural beauty – and fragrance – you can also attach cinnamon sticks, dried citrus peels or sprigs of fresh herbs such as rosemary and thyme. Use tape to secure your finished garland on the pumpkin. You could even create a smaller circle of decorated twine for its very own autumnal crown.

3. Dress to Impress

Give your pumpkin some character with props you find around the house. A scrap of fabric could be a witch's cloak or a cosy autumnal scarf. Some gauze or old white cloth might wrap it up to make a convincing mummy (don't forget the stick-on eyes peeping through). Perhaps you add a masquerade mask, tiny pointed hat, dapper bow tie or even a pair of reading glasses. Use some tape to stick any clothing or accessories in place.

4. Gothic Glamour

For a more refined look, seek out shiny satin ribbons, velvets and lace doilies to adorn your pumpkin with the textures of a vampiress' gothic home. It can be as simple as tying a few silky bows around the pumpkin's body with the help of some double-sided tape. Or, using scissors, snip a stalk-sized hole in the middle of a doily to be placed directly atop the pumpkin like a delicate headdress. With just a few swipes of your fingers or scissors, you can transform a wholesome root vegetable into something elegantly eerie.

5. Stick & Style

Keep things simple with stickers – add googly eyes, a quirky nose, expressive mouth and even some dramatic eyebrows. Or tell your own story with a cast of different characters that are dreamy, wide-eyed, evil or mischievous. Another option is to use Washi tape and scissors to make a variety of designs such as zig-zags, polka dots and stripes. Originating from Japan, this pliable decorative tape comes in many patterns and colours. Combine oranges, reds and purples for a Halloween palette or choose whatever shades your heart desires. Once your pumpkins have finished entertaining, peel your decorations off so it's ready to be cooked or composted.

The Guiding Light of the Jack-o'-lantern

The tradition of carving vegetables during Halloween is hundreds of years old, going back to the ancient festival of Samhain. Considered one of the earliest variations of the modern-day jack-o'-lantern, the Celts carved frightening faces into turnips or potatoes and then fashioned makeshift lanterns by placing a glowing ember within their hollowed-out insides. This was believed to ward off malevolent ghosts as they visited the land of the living during Halloween night. Pumpkins only gained popularity as a vessel for the jack-o'-lantern when Irish immigrants brought their Celtic traditions to North America, where they were far more plentiful than turnips.

The name jack-o'-lantern may have ties to an Irish folktale called Stingy Jack, thought to originate from the early 1600s. Jack was a drunkard and notorious trickster who seemingly outwit the Devil by securing a promise that he would never claim his soul. When Jack died, he was denied entry into Heaven on account of his nefarious ways, but the Devil stayed true to his word by also refusing him entry to Hell. Instead, Jack was doomed to wander the plane between the two realms for eternity, with only a burning coal, generously gifted by the Devil, to light his way. Jack made do with his dire circumstances, placing this measly source of light inside a carved-out turnip to make a lantern.

Though carved vegetables were not known by the name jack-o'-lantern until about the eighteenth century, the term itself was used much earlier. There are written records from the 1660s that use 'jack-o'-lantern' to describe a will-o'-the-wisp: an eerie and spectral light often witnessed over bogs, marshes and swamps at night. Also called 'ignis fatuus', which is Latin for 'foolish fire', this strange occurrence inspired folktales from Wales to Newfoundland of sprites, ghosts and other wicked beings that lure travellers deeper into the wilderness, lost forevermore. Today, the will-o'-the-wisp is known to be of natural, rather than supernatural, causes – whether from the combustion of gases from decaying plants or bioluminescence. But even a small tealight within a carved pumpkin, flickering on a doorstep during Halloween, still makes for an otherworldly sight.

Pumpkin carving remains a beloved Halloween ritual, a chance to nurture your creativity and be a little bit mischievous. As you carve, remember the centuries-long history that you are continuing… and get ready to scoop and slice your way into the Halloween spirit.

5 SIMPLE WAYS TO CARVE A PUMPKIN

But before we start, some tips!

Use the correct tools – It's best if you can get your hands on a pumpkin carving kit, which contains special knives up to the task. Otherwise, a large serrated knife will be easiest for slicing through large sections of the pumpkin's thick skin, and you can then use smaller knives for carving out shapes or perfecting intricate details. For scooping out the pumpkin brains (seeds and stringy pulp), a regular spoon or fork will do nicely.

Stay safe – When carving, place the pumpkin on a non-slip surface to prevent it from rolling or shifting as you wield your knife. You can place a damp tea towel under your chopping board for extra stability. When transforming your carved pumpkin into a lantern, using battery-operated or LED tealights is the safest option. If you do use an ordinary tealight, be mindful never to leave the open flame unattended.

A helping hand – Draw outlines of your chosen design straight onto the pumpkin skin with a marker as a guide before you start carving.

Preserve your work – After sculpting your macabre masterpiece, apply a thin layer of petroleum jelly or vegetable oil to any carved sections. This will help keep those exposed areas of the pumpkin looking fresh for longer and stop them from drying out too quickly. If using this trick, please do not use a real tealight inside the pumpkin!

* THE BARE-BONES BASICS OF CARVING A PUMPKIN *

- To make your 'lid', carefully cut around the stem to the desired size and set to one side.
- Scoop out all of the pulp, stringy bits and seeds (save the seeds for later to roast up a delicious treat, page 57).
- Once you've finished carving your chosen design, pop in your candle or LED light and secure the lid back on top of the pumpkin. Your jack-o'-lantern is done – ready to protect your home against roaming spirits or delight any mortal visitors.

1. The Classic

The jaggedy smile of this iconic pumpkin is the true face of Halloween. Catching glimpses of his mischievous grin as you pass rows of glimmering doorsteps is a treat in itself during the month of October. Start by drawing two triangle-shaped eyes, a smaller triangle nose and a wide, sharp-edged zigzag smile. You can vary these shapes a bit for some added personality – make the eyes asymmetrical or tilt the smile for some added mischief.

2. Leaves & Vines

Whether you're tracing a set of cookie cutters or the real thing, foraged from an autumnal stroll, falling leaves and vines make a beautiful natural design for your pumpkin. Using a special technique – only scraping the top layer off the pumpkin skin – you can craft an ethereal glow that will make your front door appear enchanted. Select a variety of leaf shapes and curling vines to draw around and create a stencil for your pumpkin. Using a surface carving kit or clay sculpting tool, carefully remove the outer layer of the thick skin. Work slowly to avoid cutting too deep, though the thinner you make these sections of carved skin, the brighter and more luminous the tealight will shine through. To add some details, etch dainty veins in each leaf.

3. Boo!

Carving words instead of faces is an easy but eye-catching way to spellbind your doorstep. Using alphabet cookie cutters or stencils, spell out any spooky phrase you want branded on your pumpkin. Keep it simple with 'Boo!' or a lengthier Halloween greeting such as 'Trick or Treat?'. Whether your message is cute or creepy, this playful twist on tradition will glow with eerie charm.

4. A Lick of Flames

By carving this design into the side of your pumpkin, you can either create the cosy autumn atmosphere of a warming fireplace or the roaring flames from the depths of Hell. Both are wonderfully seasonal. Using a stencil, carve tall and curling flames that wrap around the pumpkin. Carefully saw along the lines, leaving enough space between cuts for the pumpkin to maintain its structure. Once lit from within, the shivering light dances around the flame shapes – warm and welcoming or demonic, depending on your vision.

5. The Hungry Vampire

A vampire pumpkin brings two Halloween favourites together, a harmonious melding that calls forth some bloodthirsty blessings, or curses, to your abode. You can use the same eyes and nose as the classic jack-o'-lantern (though adding some high arched eyebrows would also be fabulous), and then cut a crescent mouth with two sharp fangs hanging from the top. For added bloodlust, drip some fake blood (or strawberry jam) down one side of the pumpkin's mouth.

The Seductive Smirk of a Vampire

The vampire as we know it today is a seductive creature, an alluring mix of sensuality, danger and forbidden desire. But the oldest vampiric myths contained nothing of this romanticised image. In these stories, they were grotesque beings that brought only death and decay. Early precursors to modern vampire lore can be traced back to places such as Mesopotamia, ancient Greece and India, where spirits or demons were thought to consume the life force of their victims.

It was Gothic literature popularised during the eighteenth and nineteenth centuries that immortalised the more seductive image of the vampire within its pages. These beasts were often refined, aristocratic men, such as Bram Stoker's Count Dracula. The English writer drew heavily from Romanian history and folklore, though he never actually visited the country. He was fascinated by tales of the 'strigoi', undead spirits that share many traits with vampires. Dracula's characterisation was deeply influenced by Vlad the Impaler, or Vlad Dracula, a fifteenth-century Wallachian prince who was notorious for his brutal punishments and fierce defence of his realm against the Ottoman Empire.

Stoker's vampire is a charismatic, powerful and erotically charged being who lures his victims in with a seductive smile. Being bitten is both terrifying and intimate, a sort of demonic rebirth, and Dracula's mark symbolises a deep connection that stirs up forbidden desires.

11 PERFECTLY PUMPKINY RECIPES

Pumpkins are not only a beloved staple of Halloween but also offer a wide range of nutritional benefits. Packed with dietary fibre, vitamins, minerals and antioxidants, they make a wholesome addition to your mealtimes, snacks, drinks – even your skincare regimen.

Vitamin-Rich

Pumpkins are high in vitamin A, mostly in the form of beta-carotene, which gives them their vibrant orange shade. This vitamin is essential for maintaining healthy skin, eyes and an overall well-functioning immune response. They are also rich in vitamins C and E, both powerhouses for immunity.

Many Minerals

Pumpkin seeds, sometimes known as pepitas, are particularly high in zinc, an important mineral for immunity and wound healing.

High in Antioxidants

Beta-carotene, lutein and zeaxanthin are *the* antioxidants for supporting good eye health.

Here are some pumpkin recipes to help you make this magical squash the star of your spooky season. In some of the following recipes, canned pumpkin purée is called for as the best means to deliver a dose of pumpkiny goodness. Though you are always welcome to substitute in homemade purée, be mindful that this can affect the outcome of the recipe slightly, from the texture to the level of sweetness. This is because homemade versions differ slightly in flavour and water content. But if you can't get your hands on the canned variety, no fear, a touch of seasonal spellwork (trial and error) will surely bring a positive outcome.

* PUMPKIN PURÉE *

Here's how to make a simple, natural pumpkin purée – liquid (orange) gold!

Yield — A medium pumpkin will produce about 375 to 500g of purée
Time — 1 hour 30 minutes

Ingredients

- Whatever beautiful pumpkin you source from the local farmer's market or grocery shop

Method

1. Preheat the oven to 180°C/350°F and prepare a large baking tray lined with greaseproof paper.
2. Cut your pumpkin into two halves by running a sharp knife from the top to the bottom on one side, without cutting through the tough stem. Rotate the pumpkin

180 degrees and cut the other side. Using the tip of your knife, pry open the two halves.

3. With a spoon, scoop out the seeds and stringy parts of the inner pumpkin. Set aside for making roasted pumpkin seeds (page 57).
4. Place each half on the baking tray, skin side down.
5. Bake for about 45 minutes to 1 hour, or until a fork pierces the flesh easily.
6. Rest and cool the halves for about 10 minutes, or until you can safely scoop out the softened flesh of the pumpkin. Pop the flesh into a food processor and whizz until smooth. Alternatively, use an electric mixer or mash thoroughly with a potato masher or the back of a fork.
7. Once completely cool, transfer the purée to airtight containers, seal and place in the fridge. It will keep for up to three days. The purée can also be frozen for up to three months, just make sure to pop in the freezer within two days of making it.

✱ PUMPKIN SPICE LATTE ✱

This cosy concoction is a toast to the best of the season: woolly jumpers, the warmth of sweet spices and crunching leaves beneath your boots. A velvety mugful of pumpkiny, sugary, peppery delight. Perfect for a sweet-but-spicy kick-start to the day, or the drink of choice for some afternoon reading by the fireplace.

Yield — 2 to 3 servings
Time — 10 minutes

Ingredients

- 600ml milk of choice
- 100g pumpkin purée
- 1 tsp ground cinnamon
- ¼ tsp ground ginger
- ¼ tsp ground nutmeg
- Pinch of cracked black pepper
- 1 to 2 whole cloves
- 2 to 3 tbsp sweetener of choice
- ½ tbsp vanilla extract
- 60ml strong black coffee (optional)

Toppings (optional)

- 40ml double cream, whipped until it just forms stiff peaks
- Pinch of ground cinnamon or nutmeg

Method

1. Whisk together the milk, pumpkin purée, spices and sweetener of choice in a saucepan, then warm over medium heat until the mixture begins to steam – do not bring to a boil. Make sure to stir occasionally.

2. Remove from the heat and mix in the vanilla and coffee (if using). Taste and adjust with more sweetener or flavourings if needed.
3. Remove the cloves and divide this luscious mixture between two or three mugs.
4. If you fancy some extra decadence, top with freshly whipped cream and a sprinkle of cinnamon or nutmeg.

* ROASTED PUMPKIN * WITH FETA, POMEGRANATE SEEDS & CHILLI HONEY

This dish is delectably vibrant in colour and flavour. Sweet, a little spicy, with just the right amount of salty tang. Not only does it taste heavenly, but the orange pumpkin dotted with pops of rich deep red and glistening with honey looks absolutely gorgeous too.

Yield — 4 to 6 servings
Time — 1 hour

Ingredients

- 500g pumpkin
- 3 tbsp olive oil
- 1 tsp smoked paprika
- 100g feta cheese
- 2 tbsp honey
- ½ tsp dried chilli flakes
- 50g pomegranate seeds (about a quarter of a fresh pomegranate)
- 2 tbsp fresh parsley, roughly chopped
- ½ tsp salt
- Pinch of cracked black pepper

Method

1. Preheat your oven to 200°C/390°F and line a large baking sheet with greaseproof paper.
2. Prepare your pumpkin by slicing it into two halves, scooping out the seeds and stringy bits and then cutting the flesh into cubes about 1cm (½ inch) thick.
3. Toss the pumpkin pieces with olive oil, salt, pepper and smoked paprika. Then lay them out on the baking sheet in a single layer.
4. Roast for about 30–40 minutes until the edges start to caramelise and a fork goes into the flesh easily.
5. While the pumpkin is in the oven, mix the chilli flakes and the honey in a small ramekin. Set to one side.
6. If using fresh pomegranate, deseed and place in a separate ramekin.
7. When the pumpkin is ready to come out of the oven, either transfer the pieces to a large serving dish or divide onto individual plates. Now crumble over the feta, scatter the pomegranate seeds and garnish with chopped parsley. Lastly, drizzle with the sweet-spicy chilli honey and some more olive oil.
8. Serve warm with greens for a cosy starter or side dish. You could also pair it with some grains and added protein for a beautifully balanced meal.

✱ AUTUMNAL PUMPKIN SOUP ✱

An autumnal soup that is cosy, comforting and packed with nutrients, just as all the season's delights should be. Serve up as a starter for your spooky soirée or simply keep it all to yourself for a nourishing night in. Either way, it's sure to become your go-to throughout the autumn (and winter!). Don't forget a chunk of warm, crusty bread to scoop up each and every last drop.

Yield — 4 servings
Time — 1 hour

Ingredients

- 2 tbsp olive oil or unsalted butter
- 1 onion, diced
- 3 garlic cloves, minced
- 1 tsp ground cinnamon
- ½ tsp ground cumin
- ¼ tsp ground nutmeg
- 600g pumpkin, peeled and diced
- 1 large carrot, diced
- 750ml vegetable or chicken stock
- 100ml double cream or coconut milk
- Sea salt and black pepper, to taste

Toppings (optional)

- Pumpkin seeds, raw or roasted
- A swirl of double cream or coconut milk
- Fresh coriander, roughly chopped
- A few sprigs of fresh thyme

Method

1. In a large pot, heat up the olive oil over medium heat. Fry the diced onion for about 5–8 minutes until it is slightly soft and translucent. Next, add the minced garlic, cinnamon, cumin and nutmeg. Cook for another minute until fragrant, stirring constantly.
2. Add the chopped pumpkin and carrot, cooking for about 5–10 minutes until the edges start to brown, stirring occasionally.
3. Now pour in the stock and bring the mixture to a boil before reducing the heat to let it simmer for 20–25 minutes. It's ready when the pumpkin and carrot are tender, with a fork easily piercing both.
4. You can either use an immersion blender right in the pot or transfer (in batches, if needed) to a blender and whizz until smooth. Feel free to leave it a bit chunkier if you prefer.
5. Finally, add in the double cream, salt and pepper, giving the soup one last blend. Taste for seasoning and then make adjustments.
6. To serve, ladle into bowls and garnish with your choice of toppings. A swirl of cream and sprinkling of roasted pumpkin seeds and fresh coriander is just one of the ways you can plate up this deliciousness.

✱ ROASTED PUMPKIN SEEDS ✱

After chopping or carving your glorious pumpkin, remember to keep those seeds! Packed with fibre, protein and healthy fats, these little jewels can be transformed into a delicious and nutritious snack. Roasting the pumpkin seeds unleashes their nutty flavour, which you can pair with whatever taste you're craving – salty, smoky-spicy or sweet. This customisable recipe is great to have on hand during pumpkin season.

Ingredients

Salty

For every 50g of pumpkin seeds

- ½ tbsp olive oil or melted unsalted butter
- Pinch of sea salt

Smoky Spice

For every 50g of pumpkin seeds

- ½ tbsp olive oil or melted unsalted butter
- Pinch of sea salt
- Pinch of ground cayenne pepper
- ⅛ tsp smoked paprika

Sweet

For every 50g of pumpkin seeds

- ½ tbsp olive oil or melted unsalted butter
- Pinch of sea salt
- ½ tbsp honey
- ⅛ tsp ground cinnamon

Method

1. Preheat your oven to 180°C/350°F and prepare a baking tray lined with greaseproof paper.
2. If you're using fresh seeds, scrape them out carefully and place into a sieve. Rinse them under cold water, removing any pulp or stringy bits. Before seasoning, pat them dry with a paper towel or clean hand towel.
3. In a bowl, toss the pumpkin seeds with olive oil or melted unsalted butter and whatever flavours you like. Stir to coat the seeds evenly with the oil and seasonings.
4. Lay out the seeds in a single layer on the baking tray and roast for about 15–20 minutes. Shake or stir every 10 minutes to make sure they roast evenly and don't get too browned. Keep an eye on them – seeds can burn quickly if left unattended.
5. Once the seeds are a light golden colour, remove from the oven and let them cool for about 10 minutes.
6. Serve immediately for a warm snack or leave to cool completely and store in an airtight container for up to one week.

* PUMPKIN SKIN CRISPS *

We've saved the seeds, now don't throw away those skins! All the nutritional benefits of pumpkin are also packed inside them. In fact, they are particularly high in beta-carotene, which converts into immune-loving vitamin A within the body.

Ingredients

- Cooked pumpkin, with the flesh scooped out

For every 100g of pumpkin skins, after scraping

- 1 to 2 tbsp olive oil
- Sea salt and ground black pepper, to taste
- ¼ tsp smoked paprika (optional)
- Pinch of dried chilli flakes (optional)

Method

1. Preheat your oven to 200°C/390°F and prepare a baking tray lined with greaseproof paper.
2. Once you've scooped out the pumpkin's flesh after roasting, carefully scrape away any remaining pulp or stringy bits from the inside of the skin.
3. In a medium bowl, toss the pumpkin skins in olive oil, sea salt and black pepper. For a smoky or spicy hit of flavour, add smoked paprika or a pinch of dried chilli flakes.
4. Lay out the seasoned pumpkin skins in one layer on the baking tray.
5. Roast for 10–12 minutes or until they become golden and crispy. Take care to check them every few minutes to ensure they don't burn. If the edges are getting too dark, you can flip them halfway through cooking or take them out sooner.
6. Once done, remove the skins from the oven and let them cool for a few minutes. The skins will continue to crisp up as they cool down.
7. Enjoy on their own or pair with your favourite dips – hummus, guacamole or a creamy yoghurt. They also make a wonderfully crunchy garnish for soup.

✱ PUMPKIN PIE BROWNIES ✱

These pumpkin pie brownies bring together two mouth-watering flavours and create a truly irresistible – and deliciously festive – treat. Between the rich cocoa and cinnamon-spiced pie filling, you won't be able to decide which layer is better. The answer is both together, of course!

Yield — 16 servings
Time — 6 hours (including at least 4 hours to chill)

Ingredients

Brownie Layer

- 200g unsalted butter
- 200g light brown sugar
- 50g cocoa powder
- 1 tbsp instant coffee granules (optional)
- 3 large eggs
- 70g plain flour
- Pinch of sea salt
- 1 tsp cinnamon (optional)
- 100g dark chocolate, chopped

Pumpkin Pie Layer

- 1 x 425g can of pumpkin purée (or the same amount of homemade purée)
- 200ml double cream
- 2 large eggs
- 1 tsp vanilla extract
- 150g light brown sugar
- 2 tsp ground cinnamon
- ¼ tsp ground nutmeg
- ¼ tsp ground ginger
- ⅛ tsp ground cloves

Method

1. Preheat the oven to 180°C/350°F and prepare a 23x23cm (9x9 inch) baking tray with greaseproof paper.

2. To make the brownie layer, melt the butter on low heat in a saucepan. Add the melted butter to the sugar, cocoa powder and coffee granules in a separate bowl, allowing to cool before adding in the eggs, whisk well to combine.
3. Add the flour, sea salt, cinnamon (if using) and chocolate chunks to the wet ingredients. Gently combine with a spatula, taking care not to overmix. Spoon the batter into the bottom of the baking tin.
4. To make the pumpkin pie layer – combine the pumpkin purée, double cream, large eggs, vanilla, light brown sugar and spices in a large bowl. Using a whisk or electric mixer, combine until silky smooth.
5. Using a large spoon or spatula, carefully scoop the pumpkin pie custard and spread it evenly on top of the brownie mixture. This will keep those tidy layers!
6. Bake in the oven for 50 minutes. The centre will be jiggly, but will firm up once cooled.
7. Let the pumpkin pie brownies cool completely (about 2–3 hours) before transferring to the fridge, chilling for at least 4 hours. When ready to serve, slice with a sharp knife and enjoy! Add a dollop of freshly whipped cream and dust with cocoa powder for an even more indulgent treat.
8. Store in an airtight container in the fridge for up to three days.

✱ PUMPKIN BREAD ✱

This pumpkin bread is a tender, warmly spiced loaf packed with earthy sweetness. The ultimate autumn comfort bake! It's to die for with a steaming cup of tea or strong coffee and delicious for breakfast, as an afternoon treat or even a midnight snack. It also makes a divine homemade gift for loved ones.

Yield — 9 to 12 servings
Time — 1 hour 20 minutes

Ingredients

- 250g plain flour
- 1 tsp baking powder
- ½ tsp baking soda
- 3 tsp ground cinnamon
- ½ tsp ground ginger
- ¼ tsp ground nutmeg
- ⅛ tsp ground cloves
- Pinch of sea salt
- 2 large eggs
- 175g light brown sugar
- 300g pumpkin purée
- 50ml vegetable oil
- 50g plain natural yoghurt
- 100g chocolate chips (optional)
- 15g pumpkin seeds (optional)

Method

1. Preheat the oven to 180°C/350°F and line a 25x15cm (9x5 inch) loaf tin with greaseproof paper.
2. Combine the flour, baking powder, baking soda, spices and salt in a large mixing bowl.
3. In a medium bowl, beat together the eggs and sugar, then whisk in the purée, oil, and yoghurt.
4. Using a spatula, combine the wet and dry mixtures (add the chocolate chips, if using). Don't overmix!

5. Pour this sweet orangey batter into your tin. If you fancy an added crunch, sprinkle some pumpkin seeds over the loaf.
6. Bake for 55–65 minutes. At the 30-minute mark, check to see whether the top is browning too much. If so, loosely cover your bread with some aluminium foil. You'll know the pumpkin bread is ready when a fork or toothpick comes out clean, without any wet batter sticking. Also look for a crack lengthways down the middle of the loaf.
7. Leave to cool completely before slicing.
8. Enjoy with a slathering of butter or jam. You can also pop a slice in the toaster if you'd like it warm.
9. Store in an air-tight container at room temperature for up to three days.

What if sweet treats were clairvoyant?

Barmbrack, a traditional Irish treat eaten on Halloween, is just that… or so they say. Known in Irish as báirín breac, meaning 'speckled loaf', this sweet, yeasted bread filled with dried fruits soaked in tea or whiskey might just hold the secrets to your future. This is because a trinket is baked straight into the dough, and whoever finds it in their slice is foretold a truth about their future for the upcoming year. Traditionally, these items each symbolised a different path, including a ring for marriage or a thimble for spinsterhood. To pay homage to this tradition, you could place a whole almond in your pumpkin bread. Whoever receives this slice will be blessed with good fortune, or cursed with misfortune – you decide!

✱ CHOCOLATE CHIP ✱ PUMPKIN MUFFINS

These hearty muffins are soft and sweet with a hint of autumnal spice, studded with indulgent dark chocolate. Serve in a dessert bowl paired with plain natural yoghurt and a pinch of cinnamon for an elevated snack.

Yield — 12 muffins
Time — 40 minutes

Ingredients

- 180g plain flour
- 1 tsp baking powder
- 1 tsp ground cinnamon
- ½ tsp ground ginger
- 300g pumpkin purée
- 80ml vegetable oil
- 80ml honey
- 1 large egg
- 100g dark chocolate chips

Method

1. Preheat the oven to 180°C/350°F and line a cupcake tray with twelve cases.
2. In a large mixing bowl, combine all the dry ingredients.
3. In a separate bowl, beat together the pumpkin purée, vegetable oil, honey and egg until smooth. You can use a whisk or electric mixer.
4. Combine the dry and wet ingredients and add the chocolate chips, folding the mixture together with a spatula until it just comes together. Don't overmix!
5. Spoon out the batter into each cupcake case, filling them almost to the top – don't worry, these don't rise a lot and so won't spill over.

6. Bake for 20 minutes until the edges are golden and an inserted fork comes away clean, without any wet batter.
7. Leave to cool completely or enjoy one or two warm (highly recommended).
8. Store in an air-tight container at room temperature for up to three days.

* BULGARIAN PUMPKIN PIE *

A twist (or swirl) on the classic pumpkin pie. Tikvenik is a traditional Bulgarian dessert made with sweetened pumpkin rolled in filo pastry and then shaped into a spiral. Often served during the autumn months, each mouthful of this comforting treat is filled with flavours of the season: aromatic spices, sugary grated pumpkin and buttery filo. Serve a slice at your next dinner party or enjoy as a sweet treat with a warm mugful of something just as cosy.

Yield — 8 servings
Time — 1 hour 20 minutes

Ingredients

- 1kg pumpkin flesh
- 200g golden caster sugar
- Zest and juice of 1 orange
- 2 tsp ground cinnamon
- ½ tsp ground ginger
- ½ tsp ground nutmeg
- 100ml vegetable oil, plus extra for brushing on dough
- 50g walnuts, finely chopped (optional)
- Approx. 16 filo pastry sheets
- Icing sugar (to sprinkle on top)

Method

1. Preheat your oven to 180°C/350°F and line a pie dish with greaseproof paper.
2. Grate the pumpkin and then combine with the sugar, orange zest and juice, spices and vegetable oil. Add the chopped walnuts now if using.
3. Fry this mixture in a large pan over medium heat for about 5–10 minutes, until the pumpkin starts to soften. Set to one side.
4. On a clear and dry surface, place two sheets of filo pastry ready to use first. Keep the remaining sheets covered with a clean damp kitchen towel to prevent them drying out. Brush vegetable oil on the entire top-side of the bottom sheet, and then place the second sheet over the top, again brushing the entire top-side with oil.
5. Spoon about a quarter of the pumpkin filling all over the top of the dough. Next, carefully roll it lengthways tightly into a log, tucking the edges under to keep the filling inside while baking. Twist this log into a swirl shape and place it in the centre of the pie dish. Repeat this process about four times or until the mixture is all used up, continuing the swirl outwards.
6. Brush the finished Tikvenik swirl with a final coating of oil and then bake for 30–40 minutes, or until golden brown.
7. Once done, remove the Tikvenik from the oven and allow it to cool for a few minutes before serving. Dust it with some icing sugar and then slice like a cake for your fortunate guests.
8. Once cooled completely, place in an air-tight container and keep in the fridge for up to three days.

Kukeri

Though pumpkins have no historical associations with Halloween in Bulgaria, the Balkan country has a very special tradition called Kukeri, which bears a resemblance to the holiday. Kukeri are men who dress in ornate masks and costumes of animal fur or feathers – intended to frighten malicious beings – as a way to ward off misfortune. The tradition takes place during the winter months, often between New Year and Orthodox Lent. The Kukeri dance through streets and villages, ringing large cowbells tied to their waists. This ritual brings good fortune for the upcoming year.

* NATURAL BRIGHTENING FACE MASK *

Harness the natural power of pumpkins with this homemade brightening face mask. Rich in enzymes and alpha hydroxy acids (AHAs) to gently exfoliate dead skin cells, full of zinc and antioxidants that soothe inflammation, and packed with beta-carotene to combat environmental damage, our favourite fruit is the key to a glowing complexion. Truly a goddess-send for dry and flaky faces during the colder months, it's also hydrating and gentle on sensitive skin.

Rich in lactic acid and probiotics, plain yoghurt gently exfoliates, hydrates and calms the skin. Honey is a natural humectant, so super hydrating, and an antibacterial agent, meaning it fights acne-causing bacteria, reduces redness and promotes healing.

Ingredients

- 40g pumpkin purée
- 1 tbsp plain unsweetened yoghurt
- 1 tbsp raw honey

Method

1. Mix together the pumpkin, yoghurt and honey until combined and without any clumps.
2. Wash your face with your go-to cleanser and gently dab your face dry with a clean towel.
3. Apply a thin layer of the mask to your face, avoiding the area around the eyes. Leave on for about 10–15 minutes* and then rinse well with warm water to remove. Afterwards, pop on a moisturiser to seal in that hydration and amp up the seasonal glow. If you notice any discomfort, wash the mask off immediately.

***Here are some ideas to help you unwind while the face mask works its magic**

- Do a calming breathing exercise – use the 4-7-8 method to regulate your nervous system by inhaling for four seconds, holding your breath in for seven and exhaling for eight.
- Sink into a warm bubble bath.
- Declutter your thoughts by writing a list of any worries on your mind.

SEASONAL BAKES & SWEET TREATS

Baking sweet and spooky desserts is a luscious way to ease into the season, awakening your taste buds for the bewitching days ahead. Invite some friends over to share some ghoulish graveyard chocolate mousse or gift some warming apple hand pies to your neighbours on a particularly chilly evening. Some of these have a hint of trick (meringue bones, anyone?), but all are without a doubt treats.

* SPIDERWEB CHEESECAKE *

This sophisticated vanilla cheesecake is paired with a buttery Oreo cookie crust and decorated with a dark chocolate spiderweb delicately swirled on top. An elegant and festive dessert that is surprisingly easy to make, but always a showstopper. It's the perfect way to bring a spooky finishing touch to your Halloween dinner table.

Yield — 8 to 12 servings
Time — 5 hours (including at least 4 hours to chill)

Ingredients

Crust

- 2 x 154g packs of Oreo cookies
- 75g unsalted butter, melted (plus extra for greasing)
- Pinch of sea salt

Cheesecake

- 300g cream cheese, softened at room temperature
- 100g golden caster sugar
- 1 tbsp fresh lemon juice
- 200ml double cream
- 1 tbsp vanilla extract

Decoration

- 30g dark chocolate, finely chopped
- Toothpick

Method

1. Grease a 20cm (8-inch) springform pan with plenty of melted butter.
2. Blitz the Oreo cookies in a food processor until they reach a fine crumb. You can also place them in a large sealed ziplock bag and bash them with a rolling pin.
3. In a medium bowl, combine the Oreo crumbs with the melted butter and a pinch of sea salt. Stir until the crumbs are all coated in butter.
4. Press this mixture into the bottom and around the sides of the springform pan in an even layer and place in the fridge while you make the cheesecake filling.
5. Beat the cream cheese, sugar and lemon juice in a large mixing bowl until smooth, using an electric mixer on medium to high speed.
6. In another large mixing bowl, beat the double cream and vanilla extract until stiff peaks form.
7. Taking half the mixture at a time, gently fold the whipped cream into the cream cheese with a large spoon until fully incorporated.

8. Pour this cheesecake filling over the Oreo crust and smooth out the top with the back of a spoon or offset spatula. Set aside.
9. To make the spiderweb topping, first place the finely chopped dark chocolate in a small microwave-safe bowl and heat at 30 second intervals until fully melted. Add this to a small ziplock bag, seal it and then snip off one of the corners using scissors, about 0.25cm wide.
10. Use this to pipe a swirl on top of the cheesecake, starting in the middle and moving outwards with about 1cm (½ inch) between each circle.
11. With a toothpick, drag the point from the centre to the outer edge in a straight line, repeating clockwise every 45 degrees.
12. Once your spider web is woven, place the cheesecake in the fridge to set for at least four hours, ideally overnight.
13. To serve, cut into slices and plate up.
14. Store in an airtight container in the fridge for up to three days.

✱ GRAVEYARD ✱ CHOCOLATE MOUSSE

This dessert combines the understated elegance of a classic chocolate mousse with the creepy crawly spirit of the season. The rich, creamy dark chocolate mousse is topped with dirt (crushed Oreo cookies) and wriggly (jelly) worms. An edible graveyard scene that brings just the right amount of grisly charm to your something sweet.

Yield — 4 servings
Time — 4 hours 40 minutes (including at least 4 hours for chilling)

Ingredients

Chocolate Mousse

- 4 large eggs, at room temperature
- 150g dark chocolate, at least 70% cocoa
- 1 tbsp golden caster sugar
- 1 tsp vanilla extract
- Pinch of sea salt

Toppings

- 50g Oreo cookies
- 2 extra Oreo cookies
- Approx. 12 jelly worms

Method

1. Separate the egg yolks from the whites into two bowls.
2. Melt the dark chocolate in a bain-marie* over the stove until glossy. Set aside to cool slightly.
3. Beat the egg whites using a whisk or electric mixer until they form stiff peaks.

4. Lightly whisk the egg yolks with the sugar, vanilla extract and a pinch of sea salt.
5. Next, while whisking continuously, slowly pour the melted chocolate into the egg yolk mixture until fully blended.
6. Adding about a third of the mixture at a time, combine the whipped egg whites to this chocolate mixture, folding in with a large metal spoon until you no longer see streaks of egg whites. Be careful not to overmix or you might deflate the fluffy mousse.
7. Transfer this finished mixture into four serving dishes of your choice. Refrigerate for at least four hours to set.
8. When ready to serve, split the Oreo cookies in two and scrape out the cream (no need to waste it, save as a snack for now or later), then mash the Oreo cookies in a sealed ziplock bag with a rolling pin. Sprinkle generously on top of each mousse. Slice two whole Oreo cookies in half and place each flat side down in the middle of the 'dirt' to create grave headstones. Finally, release a few jelly worms into each dessert.
9. Keep in the refrigerator for up to two days.

*Also known as a water bath, a bain-marie is used to heat delicate ingredients slowly without direct contact with high temperatures. To make one, fill a saucepan with a few inches of water and bring to a simmer. Place a heatproof bowl on top (making sure it doesn't make contact with the simmering water). Now you can add your ingredients to the warm bowl, stirring gently until melted or thickened.

* MERINGUE BONES *

These sugary bones are crispy on the outside but melt in your mouth with a burst of chewy sweetness. A classic meringue piped into a delightfully cartoonish bone shape – simple but utterly charming. They'll be a hit at any Halloween gathering.

Yield — approx. 30 bones
Time — 4 hours

Ingredients

- 6 large egg whites*, at room temperature
- ½ tsp cream of tartar
- 1 tsp vanilla extract
- 300g golden caster sugar
- 1 piping bag with a large round tip, or a large sandwich bag

Method

1. Preheat the oven to 110°C/230°F and prepare two large baking trays with greaseproof paper.
2. In a large bowl, combine the egg whites, cream of tartar and vanilla extract and whisk with an electric mixer on medium speed until frothy.
3. Gradually add in the sugar – about a tablespoon at a time – increasing the mixing speed up to high, until soft peaks form. Next, beat the mixture for about 5–10 minutes until you have stiff peaks.
4. Spoon this finished meringue into a piping bag fitted with a large round tip. Alternatively, use a sealed sandwich bag with a corner snipped off about 1cm (½ inch) wide.
5. To forge your bones, pipe straight lines that are about 2.5cm (1 inch) long, adding two heart-shape ends to

either side (with the point facing inwards). The bones can be piped relatively close together as they don't expand while cooking.

6. Bake in the oven for an hour before turning off the oven and leaving them for another 1–2 hours to cool completely.
7. Remove from the oven and store in an airtight container at room temperature for sup to three days.

***Some ways to use these leftover yolks (which can be kept covered in the fridge for up to two days)**

- Whip up a hollandaise sauce or aioli
- Make a rich custard to pair with puddings

✱ APPLE HAND PIES ✱

Enjoy the sweet comfort of apple pie in the palm of your hand. Whether enjoyed hot out of the oven with a scoop of vanilla ice cream and salted caramel sauce, or pinched as you leave the house for a tasty snack on the road, these little pies are buttery parcels of seasonal sin.

Yield — 8 hand pies
Time — 1 hour

Ingredients

- 2 large cooking apples, peeled, cored and cut into 1-inch chunks
- 70g light brown sugar
- 1 tsp ground cinnamon
- ½ tsp ground ginger
- ¼ tsp ground nutmeg
- Pinch of sea salt
- 15g unsalted butter, cubed
- 1 tbsp cornflour
- 320g ready-rolled shortcrust pastry
- 1 large egg yolk, beaten
- 2 tbsp demerara sugar

Method

1. Preheat the oven to 180°C/350°F and prepare a baking tray with greaseproof paper.
2. Mix the cornstarch with 1 tablespoon of water to make a slurry.
3. Place the apples, sugar, cinnamon, ginger, nutmeg, salt, unsalted butter and cornflour slurry into a saucepan over a medium heat and bring to a simmer for 8 to 10 minutes, stirring occasionally for 5–10 minutes until the apples soften and their juices thicken. Transfer this mixture into a bowl and set aside for ten minutes to cool.

4. Unroll the pastry sheet and cut into eight even rectangle shapes.
5. Spoon the apple mixture into one end of each pastry rectangle, leaving space around the filling to be able to seal the edges. Brush some beaten egg yolk around the edges. Now fold the other end of the pastry onto the filled half and seal the edges by crimping with the back of a fork. Taking a small knife, score a little cross in the centre.
6. Brush some beaten egg yolk over the top of each pie and then sprinkle on some demerara sugar.
7. Arrange the pies on the baking tray and bake for 15–20 minutes until the pastry is puffed up and golden brown.
8. Once baked, remove from the oven and leave to cool completely. Keep in an airtight container at room temperature for up to three days.

Soul Cakes

By the Middle Ages, which roughly spanned from the eleventh to the sixteenth century, Halloween had adopted new traditions, including 'souling'. Considered a precursor to modern day trick-or-treating, the poor would journey door to door offering prayers for departed loved ones in exchange for 'soul cakes', round shortbread-like cakes with dried fruits, sweet spices, raisins and nuts, their tops marked with a cross. While the crosses marked into these apple hand pies are to let steam escape from the buttery pastry while baking, perhaps you can emulate the tradition of souling by offering these handheld desserts to trick-or-treaters and visiting guests. If you crave something a little closer to the real soul cake, add 30g of chopped nuts and raisins to the stewed apples.

✱ WITCH FINGERS ✱

These bewitching treats are Italian ricciarelli, a chewy almond cookie made only with ground nuts, egg whites, sugar and natural flavourings. While they are traditionally oval in shape, these are rolled into finger-sized biscuits and decorated with a single almond to create some wonderfully witchy digits. Delicious with a cup of herbal tea.

Yield — approx. 40 biscuits
Time — 9 hours (including at least 8 hours for chilling)

Ingredients

- 1 tsp almond extract
- 2 large egg whites*[1]
- Zest of ½ orange
- ½ tsp dried rosemary*[2]
- 180g icing sugar
- 250g ground almonds
- Pinch of salt
- 40 whole almonds

Method

1. In a clean bowl, whisk the almond extract and egg whites for about 4–5 minutes until stiff peaks form.
2. In another clean bowl, mix together the orange zest, dried rosemary, sifted icing sugar, ground almonds and salt. Make sure everything is well combined.
3. Gently fold these dry ingredients into the whisked egg whites until they form a dough, switching over to clean hands once it starts to bind together. Cover and chill in the refrigerator for at least 8 hours, ideally overnight or for up to two days.
4. Preheat the oven to 180°C/350°F and prepare a baking tray lined with greaseproof paper.

5. Place the dough onto a work surface (dusted with icing sugar to avoid sticking). Taking quarter sections at a time, roll the dough by hand into the shape of a skinny log (they should be slightly wider than a finger) and then cut each biscuit to about 7.5cm (3 inches) in length, smoothing them out by hand to create a more 'finger-like' shape. Using a knife, score two sets of knuckle indentations into each biscuit. Finally, place an almond on the end to resemble a fingernail.
6. Bake for 10–15 minutes until the edges turn golden brown. The biscuits might crack slightly as they bake. They should appear soft when taken out of the oven but will firm up as they cool down.
7. Leave to cool completely on a rack and then store in an airtight container for up to three days.

Notes

*[1] Some ways to use these leftover yolks (which can be kept covered in the fridge for up to two days):

- Make some lemon curd, carbonara or fresh pasta.
- Brush on pastry before baking for the perfect golden finish

*[2] In herbalist traditions, rosemary is associated with protection and purification. The flavour will be subtly woodsy and floral, but feel free to omit if it's not for you

La Strega

The addition of dried rosemary to these ricciarelli honours the traditions of Italian witchcraft, known as 'stregoneria' – a practice deeply rooted in the country's folklore and religious history. The word for witch in Italian is 'strega', meaning those who were believed to possess mystical powers often linked to protection and divination. They were considered healers and often functioned as midwives in their communities, with some specialising in 'benedizioni', meaning blessings, which cleanse homes and other spaces.

La strega is a figure of spiritual wisdom and reverence who is deeply attuned to the natural world. She worked with herbs, flowers and oils to conjure up magical salves – lavender for peace, rosemary for protection, thyme for courage. You can adjust the recipe above by substituting whichever dried herb you resonate with. Buon appetito!

Part 02

RITUALS & SPELLS

For hundreds of years, Halloween was more than just costumes and candy. It was a liminal point in space and time when the veil between our world and the next became paper-thin, meaning that wayward spirits could more easily make contact with the living. As daylight hours shrink and the magical air of autumn begins to stir, this is a sacred time for profound reflection and remembrance – a chance to reconnect with the spiritual lineage of the holiday and other seasonal changes.

In this chapter, you'll discover how to harness the mystical energy that thrums this time of year, providing some rituals and spells that bring reverence to the season. This is your invitation to connect more deeply with yourself, as well as the souls that have since departed our earthly realm. With respect and intention, these quiet acts of spiritual intention can bring about beautiful transformations

HONOURING THE AUTUMN EQUINOX

Taking place on 22 or 23 September, the autumn equinox marks the time in the year when, after months of longer days, day and night are almost equal in length once more: signalling the transition from summer to autumn in the Northern Hemisphere. This time of celestial balance has been celebrated throughout cultures for millennia. For example, Michaelmas, a melding of Christian and Pagan traditions celebrated mostly in the UK, as well as the Chinese Mid-Autumn Festival, a commemoration of seasonal lunar cycles symbolised by floating lanterns and mooncakes – ornately baked dough filled with sweet red bean paste and sometimes a salted egg yolk to represent the full moon.

For Wiccans, the equinox is celebrated through the pagan festival of Mabon, one of the eight sabbats that make up the Wheel of the Year. This is a time for expressing gratitude for the harvest and honouring our relationship with nature. Rituals include feasting on autumnal foods, being at one with the earth and meditating on any resistances to change. The autumn equinox is a reminder that change is not only inevitable, but natural and wonderfully transformative. It is a period of introspection that asks us to pause and reconnect with the cycles of the natural world. Here are some meaningful ways that you can partake in observing the equinox.

✱ HOST A HARVEST FEAST ✱

Prepare a feast for friends and loved ones with a menu filled with seasonal delights such as pumpkins, parsnips and plums (see pages 49-83 for recipe ideas). Don't forget to add touches of cinnamon and nutmeg to capture the warm aromas of autumn in each mouthful. This gathering can nourish your souls as well as your stomachs if you take a moment to practise gratitude – each take turns saying what you are thankful for.

✱ GO ON NATURE WALKS ✱

Connect more deeply to the season by paying attention to the gradual transitions around you. Go on a walk through a park or forest and take note of the changing leaves as they drift towards the ground. Notice the autumnal fruits ripening even with the whisper of colder winds. By spending time outside, you can observe these shifts and be more at one with Mother Nature.

✱ RESPECT THE BALANCE ✱

As the autumn equinox marks the point when day and night briefly find equilibrium, it is the perfect time to reflect on your own internal balance. Spiritual practices such as meditation and yoga will aid this look inward. Write down any areas in your life that appear askew, but don't forget to also celebrate the harmonious! We must acknowledge both the light and darkness: only then is balance respected.

✷ SHOW GENEROSITY ✷

During this period of bounty and abundance, find ways to share and give back to others in the community. Donate to the local food bank or volunteer for a cause that is close to your heart. Just like grounding yourself in nature, these expressions of communal care are all about honouring the connections between all living things.

HOW TO SUMMON THE SPIRITS...

Building an ancestral altar is a powerful way to honour the recently departed or a longer line of ancestors. It will create a sacred space, both physical and spiritual, to reflect on your blood connection with generations before, offering gratitude for their wisdom and harnessing its protective power.

* CHOOSE A SPECIAL SPOT *

Find a quiet, tidy space within your home where you can curate a peaceful and respectful environment. This could be in a nook, on an empty shelf, atop a small table, set up in the corner of a room, or any place that feels right for you. The altar should be in a place you can visit daily and spend time comfortably in reflection, whether that's in your living room or a more private sphere, such as your bedroom.

To cleanse the space of negative energy, burn a sage stick or palo santo. Light one end and allow to burn for a few seconds before blowing out – it should start to smoulder. Pick up the other end and carefully move it around your chosen space to circulate the smoke. This purifying ritual will allow ongoing peaceful reflection. Once finished, snuff out your sage or palo santo by stubbing the lit end on the side of a heat-safe bowl.

The practice of burning sage, known as smudging, originates from Indigenous peoples of North America, and is used in purification ceremonies. Palo santo, meaning 'holy wood', comes from South America, particularly among the Inca and other Andean cultures, who burned it during rituals for healing and protection.

* ADD A PERSONAL TOUCH *

Collect old photographs, mementos and heirlooms to form the centrepiece for your altar – any personal effects that hold a strong sense of who your ancestor was and remind you of them will do. Items such as portraits, trinkets, jewellery, books, clothing, cultural artefacts or letters all work well, strengthening your connection during this reflective time. Whether you're honouring a grandparent or ancestors hundreds of years into the past, gathering these items can be a grounding exercise in and of itself.

* PROVIDE OFFERINGS & GIFTS *

From beverages to incense, these contributions are a physical gesture of respect and remembrance. Place your chosen offerings on and around the altar while expressing gratitude through spoken words or inner intentions. There are many different kinds of gifts you might include, depending on what you think best connects you to the spirits.

Food & Drink – This may include a selection of fruits, desserts or traditional dishes from your shared cultural heritage. You can also offer seasonal foods such as pumpkin, apple, cinnamon, rosemary or sage. These autumnal tastes and spices bring a touch of warmth to your offerings.

Flowers – Similarly, a favourite flower makes a thoughtful addition to an altar. Fresh, seasonal flowers evoke the beauty of life and the earth's cycles. Replace regularly to maintain their sprightly invigoration of the space.

Candles – Lightning a candle on your altar creates a warm and reverent atmosphere, welcoming in the spirits. You can choose whichever candle resonates with you most for connecting with your ancestors, from colour to scent. When lit, use the soft glow of the candle to guide your quiet reflections.

Crystals – As each crystal holds a particular meaning or spiritual property, you can customise your selection according to your wishes. For example, amethyst aids meditation and spiritual awareness, whereas rose quartz represents love and promotes emotional healing.

Here are some other crystals you can use on your altar

- Clear Quartz — clarity, protection, spiritual growth
- Black Tourmaline — grounding, power, protection
- Citrine — prosperity, joy, positivity
- Selenite — purification, harmony, healing
- Moonstone — peace, emotional balance, healing

✱ SET AN INTENTION ✱

As you are setting up your ancestral altar, and again once it's complete, take a moment to tune in to what you hope to gain from this practice. Will you ask for guidance, wisdom or protection? Do you simply want to carve out time and space to remember those who have passed? You can repeat these intentions aloud or write them in a journal. Approach each intention with respect and care – to deepen the connection with your ancestors you must nurture the spiritual bonds between you.

FULL MOON RITUALS

The full moon in October, also known as the Harvest Moon or Hunter's Moon, marks a time of abundance and transformation. It holds significance for many cultures and has inspired various agricultural traditions. Under its eerie glow, you can harness the potent energies it possesses – of change, culmination and spiritual release. This celestial power is both grounding and metamorphic. Feel the rhythms of the earth, give in to the cycles of nature and be reborn. The moon will guide you! Here are some rituals you can do to yoke its full potential.

* CREATE MOON WATER *

Place any sealed container of water outside under the radiant moonlight. As the night passes on, its potent lunar energy will be transferred to the liquid: the sacred source of life. You can use your moon water in many ways, including:

- Added to your bubble bath for added deeper relaxation
- As a cleanser to rid items in your home of negative energy
- Sprinkled over your house or garden plants
- Placed on your ancestral altar as an offering
- Brewed into a pot of herbal tea

✱ CHARGE YOUR CRYSTALS ✱

Energise your collection of crystals to enhance their spiritual properties. Before charging, consider doing a smoke cleanse with sage or palo santo to refresh their energies. Now place your crystals outside under direct moonlight. This can be in your garden, on the windowsill or in a bowl on your doorstep. Make sure to communicate positive intentions as you move through this ritual. After leaving them out overnight, retrieve your crystals and use them as usual.

✱ BREATHE A SIGH OF RELIEF ✱

The full moon, brimming with energy, offers an opportunity for a powerful cathartic release of anything that no longer serves you – old habits, toxic relationships, negative thoughts and lingering fears. This meditative exercise will help you to cut these emotional tethers so that you can enter the rest of the lunar cycle with a fresh mind.

Materials

- Candle
- Pen and paper
- Matches or lighter
- Fireproof bowl or dish

1. Sit in a comfortable spot with your candle under the light of the full moon. If inside, make sure you are by an open window for ventilation.
2. Take a piece of paper and write down everything

you want to release. This list can be as short or as long as you wish.

3. When you're ready, light the candle.
4. Carefully use this candle to catch your piece of paper alight and then leave to burn in the fireproof dish. Focus on the flame as it flickers and envision all your worries and negative thoughts melting away like the crumbling paper. With each lick of the flame, you'll feel lighter.

* INTENTION SETTING FOR THE NEXT CYCLE *

After a powerful release comes the chance to set new intentions for the following months. The heightened energy of the full moon will help bring clarity to your desires and dreams. Use this time to tune in to your hopes for the future and ask the universe for guidance on how to manifest these wishes.

Materials

- Candle
- Journal or piece of paper
- Pen
- Crystal for manifestation – such as citrine, rose quartz, clear quartz, amethyst or labradorite

1. Light your candle, finding comfort in the glowing flame. Hold your chosen crystal in your hand and pay attention to how it feels.
2. Reflect on what you want to manifest in your life for the next month. What are your goals? What dreams do you

hope to actualise? Focus on one to three changes you want to bring about.

3. Write down these intentions in a journal or on a piece of paper. Make sure to be specific about what you want to achieve.
4. Keep this note in a safe place within your home. Remember to check these intentions during the next full moon in November and reflect on your progress, always without judgement.

✱ GIVE BACK TO THE MOON ✱

As the full moon in October takes place during the harvest season, it is a wonderful time to express gratitude for physical and spiritual abundance.

Materials

- Autumn fruits, vegetables and spices, such as apples, pears, pumpkins, squash, cinnamon sticks or ginger root
- Bowl
- Candle
- Journal or piece of paper
- Pen

1. Place your selection of fruits, vegetables and spices in a bowl.
2. Find a spot inside or outside under the moonlight to take your harvest bowl and candle.
3. Light the candle and place it on the ground or a stable surface.
4. Hold the bowl of seasonal offerings and focus on the flickering candle flame. Reflect on your own harvest for this season. What have you learned? What changes have you brought forth? Consider all your blessings during the year and express gratitude for these gifts.
5. Finally, write everything down to seal the spell. Keep this note somewhere safe within your home.

JOURNALING PROMPTS

✱ 'TIS THE SEASON FOR ✱ REAPING WHAT YOU SOW

Autumn is a transitional period, one for winding down and welcoming renewal – just like the trees that shed old leaves and then blossom with the warmth of spring. Now is the time to slow down… and surrender to the call of the season.

As they say: you reap what you sow. What seeds do you want to plant? Put pen to paper to unearth any hidden desires and illuminate a greater understanding of yourself. With these journaling prompts, you can nurture the beginnings of growth so that by next harvesting season, a feast awaits you.

Some prompts are reflective, others creative, but each one will stretch your writing muscles while helping to tend your inner mind. Let's shed those old leaves and make way for healthy buds.

1. Think back to last Halloween. What are three things, big or small, you are proud to have achieved since then?
2. Which parts of yourself are you ready to shed? Which parts do you want to nurture and grow?
3. What will slowing down look like for you this season?

4. Which spooky supernatural creature would you like to be and why?
5. What sounds and scents do you associate with autumn? Perhaps the crackle of a burning wood fire or the smell of stewing apples on the stove?
6. Describe a favourite Halloween memory from childhood. How did it make you feel? How might you recapture that magic now?
7. What potion would you like to brew right now and what ingredients would it require? A pinch of cinnamon? A dash of bravery?
8. Are there any ghosts from your past that you are still having trouble letting go of?
9. Describe your perfect autumn morning.
10. Imagine lighting a candle – you are in a cosy cottage at the edge of the forest, the sun is slowly setting and casting a warm glow through the trees – what intentions are you attaching to this energy? Which developments would you like to light up in your life?

HORRORSCOPES

With the arrival of Halloween comes the end of the harvest season, and the approach of darker months – which mirrors the mysterious and unpredictable Scorpio energy that rules from late October until mid-November.

Scorpio is ruled by the planet Pluto and governs death, rebirth, power and the subconscious. Its influence during Halloween adds an emotional charge to the season, making it an ideal time for shadow work. The mysticism of the sign encourages more than mere introspection, but the dramatic shedding of old layers and confronting fears or unresolved emotions. It is a time to be reborn, for embracing the unknown and welcoming transformative growth. The synergy of Halloween and Scorpio season provides a powerful time for astrological rituals: pulling tarot cards or performing full moon magic align perfectly with the themes of letting go, honouring the past and setting powerful new intentions.

Though dark, mysterious and intense, Scorpio energy can also be adventurous and exciting. To honour both these energetic states, here is your sun sign as a horror movie trope, with a helpful seasonal suggestion. A light-hearted way to reflect on your spiritual wellbeing.

Aries (March 21–April 19)
THE MUSCLE

As the first sign of the Zodiac, Aries are natural trailblazers. But they can also be impulsive, charging full speed ahead without taking a pause to think clearly. Near the beginning of a classic slasher movie, usually a noise is heard from the creepy basement that no one has ventured into for years. Aries will grab a torch, flex their muscles and announce their decision to investigate this ominous sound. While the fearless Aries is admirable, according to the rules of horror movies, they will surely end up dead pretty quickly.

Seasonal Suggestion – Channel your fiery energy into something a little more risk-free by taking part in a Halloween escape room or midnight scavenger hunt.

Taurus (April 20–May 20)
THE SCEPTIC

Taurus is grounded and practical; it takes a whole lot to shake their belief systems. They are also pretty resistant to anything that defies logic, and so a ghost story, haunted house or cryptic warnings in a dusty old book will likely be scoffed at. A Taurus will try to explain things rationally, insisting it's all just because of a creaky floorboard or trick of the light. This means they are sometimes blind to danger until it's too late. The sceptic is often one of the first to die, stubborn in their convictions.

Seasonal Suggestion – Try to lean as much into your intuition as much as you do your logic. If a place or person feels off, don't stick around to 'prove a point'.

Gemini (May 21–June 20)

THE ACCOMPLICE

Geminis, represented by the twins, are born with a gift for duality: they are charming, clever and love to delve into philosophical discussions. In horror, the accomplice is usually the character who knows more than they let on… whispering in the villain's ear, switching allegiances or playing both sides with ease. You never quite know where they stand. Ruled by Mercury, the planet of communication and intellect, Gemini revels in shifting mindset or mood, making them the ultimate wildcard.

Seasonal Suggestion – Pen a letter to your future self, thereby embracing your dual nature: engaging the present you and the future you. Let your thoughts flow… and perhaps some insights will be unearthed.

Cancer (June 21–July 22)

THE SACRIFICIAL LAMB

The sensitive and nurturing Cancer is the emotional anchor of any group, with deep ties to family – blood or chosen. They are loyal and fiercely protective, like a mother bear defending her cubs against wolves. So they would practically jump at the chance (literally, off a cliff) to sacrifice themselves if it meant saving their loved ones. This empathy will ultimately be their undoing, but a Cancer would secretly revel in their martyrdom as they live on at the beating heart of the story.

Seasonal Suggestion — Channel your nurturing capabilities towards yourself and go for a long autumnal stroll to decompress. You have a *lot* of feelings, but try not to lose perspective by grounding yourself in nature.

Leo (July 23–August 22)

THE LEADER

Bold, confident and undeniably charismatic, they are the star athlete in the slasher movie's group of highschoolers. Leo commands attention as a natural-born leader and has an infectious energy. They also thrive on being at the centre of the action and never shy away from a challenge. Leo's bravery often inspires others, but their headstrong attitude can lead them into trouble or veer into arrogance. When faced with vengeful ghosts or killers playing mind games, this often means death for our dear Jock.

Seasonal Suggestion — Give back this season by volunteering at a charity event or spooky fundraiser. You shine brightest when your confidence uplifts others.

Virgo (August 23–September 22)
THE SERIAL KILLER

Methodical, detail-oriented and always three steps ahead, Virgo's sharp mind and analytical nature make them the perfect match for this chilling character. Their quiet intensity and need for perfection hides a darker side – a fascination with the psychology of power, control and hidden patterns. Like the most unsettling horror villains, Virgo can play the long game with unnerving calm.

Seasonal Suggestion — Bury your perfectionism in the grave, Virgo. This Halloween, let yourself revel in some spontaneous fun by dressing up and going out without planning every single detail.

Libra (September 23–October 22)
THE FLIRT

Ruled by the planet of love, Venus, the charming and magnetic Libra can't help being so enticing. They thrive in social settings and possess a gift for connection – perhaps a little too much. Libra is likely to get distracted by anyone that catches their eye and might indulge in some R-rated fun, even amidst a crisis. In slasher movies, if you have sex, you die… a trope that reflects rather conservative views about which kinds of women are deemed worthy of living (meanwhile, the Final Girl is typically more virginal and adverse to 'bad' behaviour).

Seasonal Suggestion — Your sensual side is a beautiful thing. Head to a lively bar or costume party with your friends.

If someone catches your eye, flirt away! Embrace pleasure without shame.

Scorpio (October 23-November 21)

THE RED HERRING

Scorpio's intense and mysterious energy make them a natural fit for the horror movie villain, or so you suspect. They already seem like they're hiding a deep, dark secret and any alibis they offer up are vague at best. Everything points to them! But then, when the big reveal comes, the killer is someone else entirely – someone totally unexpected. Except, now that you think about it, that also makes sense. Scorpio really does make a fabulous red herring.

Seasonal Suggestion – Reveal more of yourself this season and invite your close friends over for a tarot card reading. Get a load off your chest by baring some secrets to your trusted inner circle.

Sagittarius (November 22-December 21)

THE LONE WOLF

Bold, confident, someone who forges their own path... though this often means wandering away from the safety of the group to face the danger (possessed doll) alone. Independent and free-spirited, Sagittarius trust their instincts and don't feel bound by social rules or what's expected of them. Though their solitary nature puts them at risk in a horror movie, their courage and resourcefulness usually sees them survive against the odds. They might disappear for chunks at a time but turn up just when you need them most.

Seasonal Suggestion – Run with the pack this Halloween and commit to some dedicated teamwork by organising an elaborate murder mystery party with friends.

Capricorn (December 22–January 19)

THE FINAL GIRL

Capricorn is logical, responsible and often has a no-nonsense attitude that makes them the ideal candidate to take the lead in a crisis, i.e. when a maniacal axe-wielding killer is on the loose. While others are screaming their heads off or paralysed with fear, Capricorn has already hatched up an escape plan. Their industrious spirit will probably see them through until they're the last one standing.

Seasonal Suggestion – Capricorn, sometimes (all the time) you're a little too serious. Be more carefree by wearing a nonsensical costume and eating far too many sweets. Your dentist will forgive you.

Aquarius (January 20–February 18)

THE GUIDE

The quirky and independent Aquarius would easily play the eccentric character who lives on the outskirts of town, offering cryptic advice and warning others of impending doom every other week. They have an unconventional way of thinking that means they often aren't taken seriously at first. People will dismiss their ramblings, until it's too late. As the mystery unfolds, their strange wisdom becomes the key to survival.

Seasonal Suggestion – Though you are naturally a bit of a hermit crab, immerse yourself in community this Halloween by baking some spooky sweet treats to hand out to neighbours and loved ones.

Pisces (February 19–March 20)
THE SEER

Pisces are deeply intuitive and in touch with their emotions. They so often feel things more strongly than others, it's as if they exist on another plane altogether. In a horror movie, they are the one who starts to experience prophetic dreams and visions or can communicate with the spirit in a haunted house. Pisces may appear dreamy and detached, but they are closely attuned to the energies that others overlook.

Seasonal Suggestion – Let your intuition guide some personal insight by keeping a dream journal each night. What is your subconscious trying to tell you?

TAROT PROMPTS FOR EERIE REFLECTIONS

Believed to have originated in Renaissance-era Italy, the tarot was once just a humble set of playing cards. It evolved into its mystical form by the eighteenth century, when it was used to channel divination and spiritual guidance. According to occultists, these seventy-eight-card decks, with each card holding a unique meaning, could unearth personal truths that help you connect more deeply with your experiences.

Today, tarot still offers a medium through which to gain valuable insight into our psyches. Below are some prompts and spreads, inspired by this eerie time of year, to help you tap into the mysterious energy that surrounds us.

✱ HOW TO SELECT CARDS ✱

Choosing tarot cards is a personal and highly intuitive process that connects the reader to the deck, bringing about a heightened state of focus on the question at hand. Here's a quick guide to help you draw your cards with intention and clarity.

✱ PREPARATION ✱

1. **Get Your Space Ready** — Find a quiet and comfortable area where you can focus without any distractions. You can light a candle or burn some incense to help channel your frame of mind.
2. **Focus Your Intention** — Before you start, take a few minutes (or however long you need) to ground yourself and get present. Think about the question you intend to ask or the area of your life you hope to gain insight into.
3. **Shuffle the Cards** — There is no 'correct' way to shuffle your cards – whatever feels natural to you is what's right. You can shuffle them like playing cards or even lay them out on a flat surface and mix them around in a messy manner. Just keep focusing on your intention or question as you shuffle, continuing until you feel a sense of completion. Trust your gut.

✱ SELECTION ✱

There are two popular options for drawing cards…

Cut the deck – Once you feel ready, hold the deck in one hand or both hands. While focusing on your question, use one hand to cut the deck into as many piles as the spread requires. For each cut, the bottom card is your selection.

Fan out – After laying your deck on a flat surface, gently use your hand to spread the cards out in a wide arc. You can adjust them slightly if you want to even out the spread. Again, whatever feels right. Now draw the number of cards needed for your chosen spread by hovering your fingers over them, or even touching the cards, letting your intuition guide you.

If any cards pop out while shuffling, include them in the spread! They could be providing an urgent message. Similarly, if any selected cards are upside down (reversed), make a note as this changes their meaning.

* READ & REFLECT *

Lay out the cards in the order for each given prompt. Using online resources, interpret their meaning based on their position in the spread and what they might reflect back about your life. Take time to journal your readings so you can note any recurring cards or messages.

These prompts are a beginner-friendly way to facilitate deeper reflections on the shadowy corners of your mind: illuminating unanswered questions and providing guidance for moving past any spiritual blockages.

✱ AN ANCESTOR'S CALL ✱

This one-card pull will help you connect with the wisdom of your ancestors. It invites you to tap into the lessons learned throughout your lineage and embrace insights from those before you. Perhaps you need to acknowledge some ongoing generational cycles, or require a guiding hand from a lost loved one. This will help you become closer to your ancestral roots, but it is also a supportive practice in this season of transition and transformation.

Prompt – If I could receive a message from an ancestor, what would they want me to know?

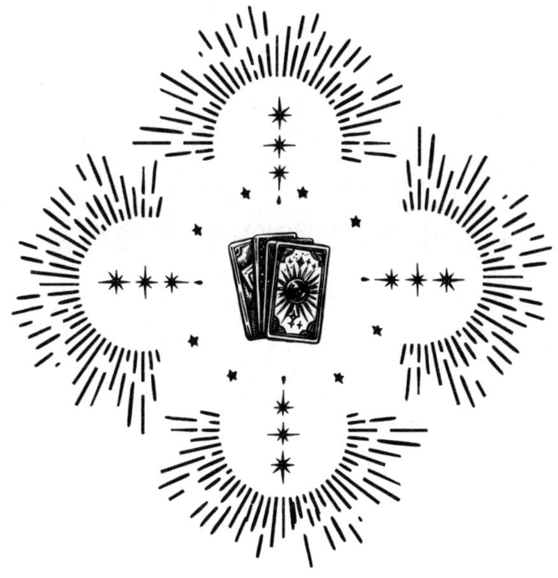

✱ TRICK OR TREAT ✱

Are you a trick or treat? *Trick* question: there is no fixed sense of self! We all wear masks in our daily life to make us feel that we belong. While this mechanism can be protective, sometimes these masks become too comfortable and hold us back from accepting the truth or moving on from an outdated version of ourselves. This spread brings clarity on your own identity, providing a non-judgemental space for accepting harder truths while acknowledging the ways you are thriving.

(1) – Trick: What mask am I hiding behind?
(2) – Treat: Which part of myself feels free and unashamed?

✱ GHOST OF YOUR PAST ✱

Oftentimes, there are ghosts from our past that continue to haunt the present, whether we realise it or not. As the veil between the departed and living is thinnest during Halloween, now is the time to make contact with these foregone ghosts and finally make peace with them. Reflect on any outdated beliefs or behaviours connected to these spirits, lingering on. Once you meet them face to face, you are given a chance to let go, move on and thrive.

(1) A ghost from my past
(2) How it is still haunting me
(3) How I can release its grip

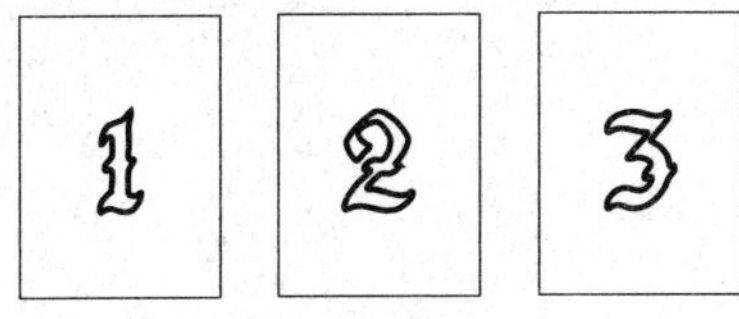

✱ PUMPKIN PATCH ✱

This spread asks you to tend to your own spiritual pumpkin patch. Tackling past, present and future, it guides you through a comprehensive look at your life. How can you grow your most healthy and plump pumpkins? These 'pumpkins' can represent whatever resonates most for you – successes, milestones, relationships or new skills. Now is the time to cultivate your own abundance. A bountiful harvest awaits you!

(1) Old roots that need to be pruned
(2) An area in my life that requires growth
(3) Which pumpkin (blessing) does my heart desire most?
(4) What I must do to ensure a fruitful harvest in the future

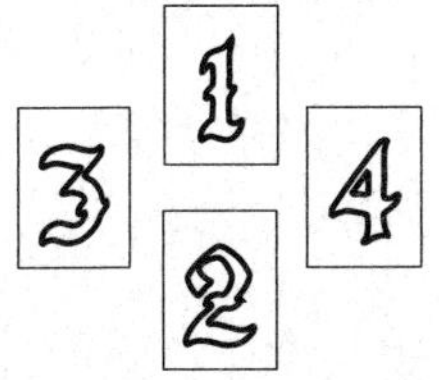

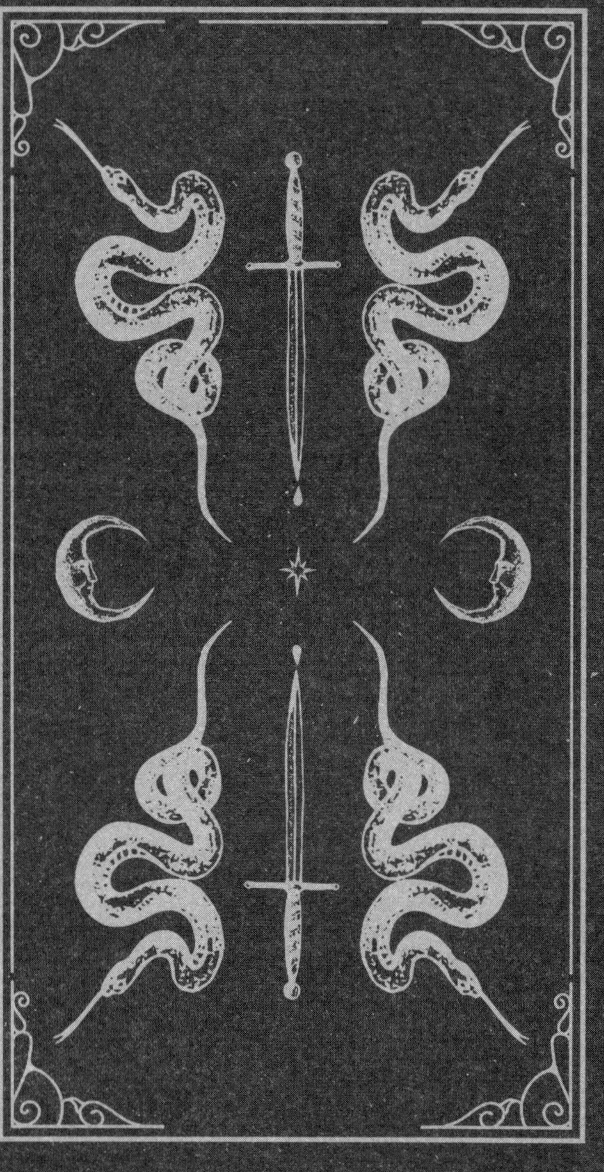

Part 03

HOW TO HOST

Spooky season is best spent surrounded by loved ones and kindred spirits, whether for a cosy and nourishing weeknight dinner or a fanciful costume party. Hosting is a chance to embrace both magic and mischief. It's about fashioning an eerily enchanting atmosphere that your guests will never forget. How can one perfect this ambiance?

You want to bring the whimsical air of the season – leaves rustling, mysterious masked faces and the shiny glaze of candy apples – right into your home.

This chapter will help you undertake this transformation, showing you how to decorate your space and charm your guests with the flick of a wand.

SPOOKY DÉCOR & CRAFTS

Harness the mystical energy of Halloween by shapeshifting your home into a haven of spooky delights. Evoke the reverence of the season with a handcrafted bouquet for the undead or pour your very own soy candles, inspired by the rich scents of autumn. Taking the time to revamp your nest with homemade decorations and trinkets is a form of spellwork – foraging, crafting and creating all bring you closer to the spirit of the season.

Whether you're hosting a wild Halloween party or simply want to surround yourself with beautifully macabre things made by hand, these pieces will surely ignite your inner witch. Better yet, invite your friends, old or new, for a crafting session and make magic together.

✱ A HALLOWEEN WREATH ✱

Both Halloween and autumn remind us to seek beauty in decay and honour the cycle of life and death. Making a Halloween wreath with foraged materials is both environmentally friendly and a means to ground yourself this season. Tune in to the flows of the earth by noticing every browning leaf drifting in the breeze, little twig underfoot and scattered conker as you potter through your garden or the park. Whether an iridescent fallen feather or the flash of a burnt orange leaf, pop whatever spoils of the season draw your attention in your pocket or bag for later. With your collection of nature's offerings in tow, you can pay tribute to Halloween in the most bewitchingly rustic way, starting with your front door.

Materials

- Wreath base or frame
- String, twine or craft wire
- Scissors or garden clippers

Ideas for decorating

- Dried leaves
- Pinecones
- Acorns
- Conkers
- Twigs
- Dried flowers and sprigs of herbs
- Feathers (that have naturally fallen)
- Cinnamon sticks
- Dried citrus slices
- Satin or velvet ribbons
- Spooky trinkets and jewellery

1. Set aside a few hours to forage for your materials, or do so over a few days. Search in your own garden, the local park or on a long forest walk. Collect your items in a wicker basket or tote bag.
2. Arrange your foraged pieces in the shape of the wreath base to give yourself a rough idea of how it will come together. Start with foliage, leaves and twigs to create a solid base before layering on some smaller or more unique items over the top. Tuck leaf stems into the wreath to keep them firmly in place and use string or craft wire to secure any larger items. When decorating, follow either a clockwise or anticlockwise direction for a smoother look or leave it more untamed if you'd prefer it to evoke the wilderness.
3. Once you've finished, add a loop of strong twine or thick ribbon to the top and use this to hang your wreath on your front door or above the fireplace. Over time, it might naturally weather and fade, which only adds to its autumnal beauty. A daily reminder of the changing seasons, and the sense of renewal they bring.

✱ A BOUQUET FOR THE UNDEAD ✱

While the thinning veil between the physical and spirit world on Halloween has long evoked a fear of malicious ghosts, it also presents a time for remembering those who have passed on. This bouquet for the undead pays respects to this magical time of year, when spirits can walk among us, and brings some eerie yet elegant charm to your home.

Materials

- Vase
- Scissors or garden clippers
- Seasonal fresh flowers
- Dried flowers
- Sprigs of fresh herbs
- Feathers (fake or naturally fallen)
- Lace, velvet and ribbons
- Antique jewellery

1. Clean your chosen vase and fill halfway with fresh water. If you have flower food, empty the sachet into the vase and give it a quick stir.
2. Cut the stems of any fresh flowers at 45 degrees and trim off any leaves that will fall below the waterline once in the vase.
3. When arranging your flowers and decorations, start with a good foundation of foliage to provide structure. You can criss-cross flower stems to give them more support. Jewellery and smaller items can be hung from sturdier stems or wedged between them.
4. For the colour palette, black, red and deep purple are suitably gothic, but choose whatever flowers speak to you.

Dried varieties such as lavender and baby's breath have a spectral quality that look beautiful. You could also include sprigs of fresh herbs such as rosemary or thyme for an earthy feel.

5. To incorporate more textures and bring your deathly bouquet to life, add feathers, strips of lace or some antique jewellery.
6. Once finished, tie some ribbon or velvet around the vase neck for an elegantly antique finishing touch.

Día de los Muertos

Día de los Muertos, or Day of the Dead, is a Mexican holiday celebrated on 1 and 2 November, rooted in both ancient Aztec and Catholic traditions, with the latter introduced by Spanish colonists in the sixteenth century. On this day, spirits of the deceased are invited by their loved ones for a fleeting reunion. This is no sombre affair, but rather a vibrant reaffirmation of life.

To welcome back their dearly departed, families will adorn altars, known as 'ofrendas', with flowers, candles, photographs, sugar skulls and food. Homes are gleaming with colour and candlelight as people gather to reminisce. While the traditional flowers used are the Mexican marigold, or cempasúchil, this bouquet for the undead echoes the spirit of joyous reverence that Día de los Muertos holds.

✱ MAKING ART WITH FALLEN AUTUMN LEAVES ✱

As the trees surrender their cloaks of old leaves, getting ready for new growth in spring, capture the wild soul of autumn by making art with foraged fallen leaves. As you collect, admire the ephemeral beauty of the unfurling season. By honouring trees in this way, you harmonise your creative energy with the slowing pulses of fall.

First, We Forage

With a bag slung over your shoulder, venture into the woods or take a quiet stroll through the park, minding each step to look for falling or fallen leaves. Seek out vibrant and earthy colours, intricate vein patterns and charming imperfections. Maple leaves have eye-catching reds while the oak tree sheds bronze leaves tinged with gold. Choose a dry day for foraging, and make sure to avoid anything wet or soggy.

Leaf Rubbing & Painting

These are simple yet enjoyable ways to admire nature's endless varieties while creating something artistic. When rubbing, the texture and pattern of each leaf will appear like a ghostly imprint through the paper, while using leaves as natural paintbrushes brings your focus to their intricate designs. Select colours that match the earthy tones of your foraged leaves.

Leaf Rubbing

Materials

- Fallen leaves
- White or coloured paper
- Crayons

1. Place a leaf or selection of leaves vein-side-up under a sheet of white paper.
2. Remove the paper peel from your chosen crayon or crayons, and then use the side of it to gently rub over the paper with the leaves underneath.
3. Overlap leaves for interesting crossover patterns or experiment with layered colours.
4. Once finished, display your autumnal art in a wooden frame or use it as a homemade greeting card. To give it more support, glue the leafy paper on some thicker card of the same size, and then fold in half.

Leaf Painting

Materials

- Fallen leaves
- Acrylic paints
- Canvas paper

1. Dip the edges or veins of each leaf into the paint, then press them firmly onto the canvas paper to transfer unique stamps and marks.
2. Experiment by layering different leaves or colours on top of each other, building depth and texture.
3. Once finished, let the painting dry completely for at least twenty-four hours before framing or hanging up in your home.

✷ CAST A SPELL OF LONGEVITY ✷

Pressing leaves is a simple way to preserve their colour and shape, turning autumn finds into lasting keepsakes. Properly dried, they can last for several years! Just be sure the leaves you collect are completely free of moisture before pressing, as dampness can lead to mould.

Materials

- Fallen leaves
- Newspaper or greaseproof paper
- Heavy book

1. Place your leaves between two sheets of newspaper or greaseproof and then lay under a heavy book. You can also use any heavy object that covers the surface area of the leaves.
2. Leave them pressed for about one to two weeks to ensure they dry out completely and flatten. Check occasionally for mould – if you encounter any, discard that leaf.
3. Once fully dried, your pressed leaves can be used for crafts, decorations or simply kept safe between the pages of a diary.

✱ LEAFY LANTERNS ✱

Using newly pressed leaves, call forth a seasonal ambience within your home with these lovely handcrafted lanterns.

Materials

- Pressed fallen leaves
- An empty mason jar
- Non-toxic PVA glue
- A small paintbrush
- LED tealight

1. Collect fallen leaves in a variety of shapes and colours, as many as you need to cover the surface of your mason jar. Avoid brittle leaves as they'll fall apart too easily.
2. Fill a small plastic container with PVA glue and water at a ratio of 1:1. Mix until smooth.
3. Using the paintbrush, apply a generous layer of glue to the section of the jar where you want to place your first leaf. Press this leaf onto the glued section, making sure the underside is smoothed down, and hold it gently for a few seconds to help it stick. Next, brush another layer of glue over the top of the leaf. Repeat the process until you have added all your leaves in the pattern you wish.
4. Once all leaves are glued in place, apply a final layer over the entire outer surface of the jar to seal everything and create an even, slightly frosted finish.
5. Leave to dry for at least four hours or overnight. Once it's completely dry, tie some string or ribbon around the neck of the jar as a finishing touch and then pop in a tealight. Now you can admire the glowing autumnal colours and textures.

DIY DECORATIONS

1. A Garland of Spider Legs

Add some spine-tingling adornments to your home with a garland of inky-black spiders, made only from card.

Materials

- Black card
- Pencil
- Scissors

1. Fold the piece of black card in half lengthways and then cut along the seam to create two strips.
2. Take one of these strips and fold it in a back-and-forth accordion-style, making sure each fold is the same width.
3. On the top fold of the accordion, draw half of a spider shape as if down the middle. Ensure that the spider's legs extend to the edge of the fold. This design will allow the spiders to connect together when the paper is unfolded.
4. Carefully cut along the lines of your spider shapes. Be cautious not to cut through the folded edge where the legs touch.
5. Gently unfold the paper to reveal a chain of spiders. If you want a longer garland, repeat the process with other strips of card and then connect multiple chains by gluing or stapling the ends together.

6. Once your spiders are finished, hang across windows, mantles or on the wall with a bit of tape. For some extra spook, use a red marker or glitter pen to dab a pair of gleaming scarlet eyes to each spider.

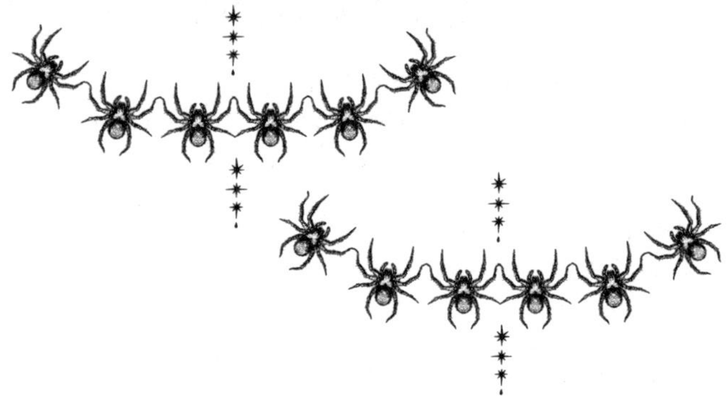

2. A Witch's Broomstick

Using natural supplies, you can craft your very own besom, or witch's broom, a traditional symbol of protection that sweeps away negative energy. It's a charming piece to keep around the house, and very useful for a quick tidy up.

Materials

- 1 sturdy branch or stick, approx. 1m long
- A bundle of thinner twigs
- Scissors or secateurs
- String or twine

1. Collect fallen branches and twigs – never break living ones. Look for dry, flexible twigs and a strong, sturdy branch for the handle.

2. Trim the twigs to a uniform length for the broom head and strip away any leaves or smaller offshoots. Gather the twig bristles and fan them out around one end of the handle. Now tightly wrap string or twine around the twig bundle, binding it firmly to the stick. Wrap several times and knot securely.
3. You can also decorate with dried herbs or velvet ribbons for an even more mystical look.

3. Paper Pumpkins

These sweet and whimsical paper pumpkins evoke memories of cosy autumn afternoons. Easy to make with just a few materials, they'll be popping up all over the place – a papery pumpkin patch.

Materials, for 1 small pumpkin

- Orange construction paper
- Scissors
- Glue stick
- Hole punch
- Brown paper
- Green pipe cleaner

1. Cut your orange paper into four strips, each about 2.5cm (1 inch) wide.
2. Then glue two strips together at the centre to form a cross shape.
3. Glue the remaining two strips diagonally, evenly spaced to form eight 'slices' of your pumpkin.

4. Use a hole punch to make a puncture near the end of each strip, about 0.5cm (¼ inch) from the edge.
5. Cut a small rectangle of brown paper for the stem. Roll it into a cigar shape, ensuring one end fits through the punched holes. Secure it with glue or a bit of tape.
6. Next, lift one strip and insert the narrow end of the stem through its hole from underneath.
7. Moving clockwise, lift the next strip, apply a bit of glue around its hole, and then slide the stem (with the first strip) through both holes. Press gently to adhere.
8. Repeat this process, moving around the circle, until all strips are gathered by the stem, forming a pumpkin shape.
9. Lastly, bend a green pipe cleaner into wavy tendrils or leaves and cut in half. Insert each one into the hole by the stem to complete your paper pumpkin.

4. A Collection of Potion Bottles

Perhaps you already have a stash of empty glass jars and trinket bottles, otherwise, keep your eye out next time you're at the vintage store or charity shop. Find a variety of shapes and sizes – any with a cork stopper or ornate detailing are particularly witchy.

Materials

- Glass jars and bottles, with lids
- Water
- Food colouring
- Dried flowers, herbs or foraged items (optional)
- Labels
- Pen
- String or ribbon

1. Fill each of your containers with water.
2. Next, decide on the colours for each potion – the deepest black, a ruby red or amber? Depending on the size of the jar or bottle, add a few drops of food colouring or natural dyes until you get your desired shade.
3. You can also add in dried flowers, herbs and little foraged items for a wild or earthy look.
4. For a fanciful detail, write your desired potion name or effect on a brown label, attaching to the jar or bottle neck with some string.
5. Proudly display your collection of potions on a shelf, windowsill or even your dining table.

5. Citrus Hangings

Creating a hanging of dried citrus slices is a simple and fragrant way to add a touch of natural beauty to your home. With some autumnal sun, the light will shine exquisitely through the translucent segments of the citrus fruits, like jewels.

Materials

- Three to five citrus fruits
- String or twine
- Toothpick or skewer
- Small charms or beads (optional)

1. Preheat the oven to 90°C/190°F and prepare a baking tray with greaseproof paper.
2. Slice your citrus into thin, even ¼-inch thick rounds. Put them on the tray in a single layer and bake in the oven for 2–3 hours, flipping halfway, until fully dehydrated and dry to the touch. Let them cool completely.

3. Arrange your slices into vertical lines with as many as you want on each hanging, leaving roughly 1cm (½ inch) between each slice.
4. Measure out lengths of string or twine that are the same length as your citrus rows with about 5cm (2 inches) extra at the top and bottom (for knotting).
5. Move your string up through each citrus slice by poking small holes at the bottom and top of each one with a toothpick or skewer.
6. If you'd like to add some charms or beads to the bottom and top of your hanging, you'll need to tie a double knot at the bottom first to support the accessory. You can then thread each slice top to bottom, tying another double knot for the final accessory to sit on.
7. Once you've finished, tie a double knot at the bottom and a loop at the top.
8. Repeat this process until you run out of slices.
9. Hang your citrusy hangings across doorways, over a mantel or against the wall using a bit of tape.

* HAND-POURED * SEASONAL CANDLES

There's something so magical about flickering candlelight during Halloween. These candle blends combine the four elements, grounding your senses and evoking the mystical power of Mother Earth during this transitional period. Their warm glow and enchanting scents invite reflection, calm and a deeper connection to the natural world.

Materials, for one candle

- 125ml glass jar or tin
- Pre-waxed cotton wicks with holding tabs
- Wick holder (chopsticks or lolly pop sticks can be used instead)
- Wick sticker or hot glue
- 100g soy wax flakes
- Wax thermometer
- Essential oils

Scents

Rain-Soaked Earth

- 20 drops vetiver
- 15 drops lemongrass
- 10 drops patchouli

Moon Water

- 20 drops rose
- 15 drops chamomile
- 10 drops lavender

Autumn Air

- 15 drops cedarwood
- 15 drops cinnamon leaf
- 10 drops vanilla

Crackling Fire

- 20 drops cedarwood
- 15 drops sweet orange
- 10 drops clove

1. Clean and dry your chosen container.
2. Use a wick sticker or a dab of hot glue to secure the wick in the centre of the bottom of the jar. Use a wick holder to keep the wick upright and centred when you start pouring the candle.
3. On a low heat, melt the wax in a bain-marie on the stove, stirring occasionally with a spatula. Once melted, continue to heat the wax until it reaches 85°C/185°F*. Set aside and cool to about 60°C/140°F.
4. You can now add in your essential oil blend. Stir for 1–2 minutes to ensure even distribution.

5. Carefully pour the scented wax into your prepared jar, leaving about 1cm (½ inch) of space at the top. Avoid moving the wick.
6. Let the candle cool undisturbed for 12–24 hours.
7. To decorate, tie twine, ribbon or lace around the neck of your jar. You can also attach a label with its name and scent, handwritten in ink.
8. For a stronger scent, allow the candles to cure for at least 48 hours but ideally one week before lighting. The burn time will be roughly 20–30 hours.

*Double check the heating instructions for your wax, as each manufacturer is slightly different. They will also give an ideal temperature for adding fragrance or essential oils.

How to Safely Burn Your Candle

- Always burn on a heat-safe and stable surface.
- Trim the wick to 0.5cm (¼ inch) before lighting.
- Never leave it unattended.
- Do not burn for more than 1–2 hours at a time.
- Extinguish the flame with a candle snuffer.

SEASONAL GATHERINGS

Spooky season is best spent surrounded by loved ones and kindred spirits, whether for a cosy and nourishing weeknight dinner or an eccentric costume party.

* PLAYLISTS *

Cosy & Mystical

The soundtrack for tranquil dinners or hosting autumnal crafting sessions.

1. Spooky – Dusty Springfield
2. I Put a Spell on You – Nina Simone
3. Season of the Witch – Lana Del Rey
4. Sisters of the Moon – Fleetwood Mac
5. Monster Mash – Bobby 'Boris' Pickett
6. Jeepers Creepers – Jack Teagarden
7. Tonight You Belong to Me – Patience and Prudence
8. 'Tis Autumn – The King Cole Trio
9. September in the Rain – Dinah Washington
10. we fell in love in october – girl in red
11. Cemetry Gates – The Smiths
12. Rhiannon – Fleetwood Mac
13. Black Magic Woman – Santana
14. zombie girl – Adrianne Lenker

15. Halloween – Phoebe Bridgers
16. I Wish I Was the Moon – Neko Case
17. Frank Sinatra – Witchcraft
18. That Old Black Magic – Ella Fitzgerald
19. Bad Moon Rising – Creedence Clearwater Revival
20. Witchy Woman – Eagles

Spirited & Spine-Tingling

For throwing the best Halloween house party of the season.

21. bury a friend – Billie Eilish
22. Evil Woman – Electric Light Orchestra
23. Witches – Alice Phoebe Lou
24. Teenage Witch – Eels
25. Superstition – Stevie Wonder
26. Psycho Killer – Talking Heads
27. Zombieboy – Lady Gaga
28. Night Crawling – Miley Cyrus ft. Billy Idol
29. Pet Sematary – Ramones
30. Vampire in the Corner – Magdalena Bay
31. Somebody's Watching Me – Rockwell
32. Maneater – Nelly Furtado
33. Disturbia – Rihanna
34. Bad Romance – Lady Gaga
35. Heads Will Roll – Yeah Yeah Yeahs
36. Thriller – Michael Jackson
37. Ghostbusters – Ray Parker Jr.
38. Little Dark Age – MGMT
39. Haunted – Beyoncé
40. Vampire – Olivia Rodrigo

TABLESCAPING IDEAS FOR A SPOOKY SOIRÉE

Elevate candlelit dinners or autumn harvest brunches with these tablescaping themes and ensure that your spooky soirées are imbued with seasonal whimsy and spellbinding detail.

1. Dark & Mysterious

A chic and sophisticated setting that evokes gothic elegance. Entice your guests with dark, rich colours and embellished details. Use a tablecloth that's black as night or a white lace runner for a charmingly vintage feel. Lay out plenty of antique accents – candlesticks in ornate holders or trinkets you've picked up at the flea market. Think skulls, ravens and ornate keys. Black cotton napkins with silver rings and dark flowers such as burgundy roses or deep red dahlias will add a stylish finishing touch to your table. Remember to serve plenty of red wine for a decadent evening with your secret circle.

2. A Charming Pumpkin Patch

For a softer, more cosy autumnal setting, draw inspiration from the harvest season to bring the spirit of abundance to your table. From cotton tablecloths to ribbons, adorn your table with different shades of orange, brown and yellow to emulate fallen leaves and ripening winter squashes. Tie napkins with pieces of twine for a rustic look and, real or fake, dot some small pumpkins and squashes in the middle of your table as a festive centrepiece. Bunches of wheat, cinnamon sticks, acorns and foraged autumn leaves can be scattered around the table, adding texture and a heavenly earthy fragrance. By incorporating these natural elements, you can pay tribute to the season in the best way possible – having loved ones join you for a delicious feast on a bountiful table.

3. The Witch's Invitation

Begin with a deep purple or midnight blue tablecloth and seek out other patterns with silver moons and constellations. Display crystals, tarot cards and antique potion bottles for the enchanted look of a witch's study. You can scatter dried herbs like lavender or rosemary across the table to cast spells of tranquillity and healing. Use plum or indigo napkins with metallic rings and celestial charms. Layers of sheer black tulle or velvet will bring some texture and a hint of mystery. Don't forget to garnish the table with plenty of candles to cast a magical glow over your guests. The kind of atmosphere that nurtures an enlightening tarot reading with your coven.

WAYS TO FOLD A FEARSOME NAPKIN

1. Guardians of the Night

With only a few folds a humble black napkin will transform into a flying bat.

1. Lay out the napkin on a flat surface so that one corner is pointing upwards. Fold the napkin in half, bottom to top corner, keeping it as even as possible.
2. Now that you have a triangle (with the longest edge on the bottom), fold the napkin in half again by bringing the right corner across to meet the left one.
3. Rotate the napkin so the 90° angle is pointing downwards.
4. To form the bat's head, fold this 90° angle up so that a small triangle peeks over the edge at the top.
5. Using the centre point along the bottom as a guide, fold the right wing at a 45° angle. Repeat on the other side.
6. To add some more details to the head, fold the middle point about 1cm (½ inch) and then create a small dent in the centre to shape some pointy ears.
7. Repeat these steps for as many bat napkins as you need – soon you'll have your very own army of darkness.

2. A Ghostly Table Presence

Take some white napkins, cotton or paper, place a rolled-up ball of paper at the centre of each and then enclose the napkin around it, tying it together with a piece of string or ribbon. This is a quick and easy way to call forth a floating ghost to keep your dinner guests company.

The Hungry Ghost Festival

Known as Zhongyuan Festival in China and Phor Tor in parts of Southeast Asia, the Hungry Ghost Festival has its origins in Buddhist and Taoist traditions. Taking place during the seventh month of the lunar calendar, referred to as the 'Ghost Month', the celebration occurs when it is believed that the gates to the afterlife are open, allowing wandering spirits to make their way to Earth. To appease these restless souls, families will make offerings, including food and the burning of joss paper, to relieve spirits of any financial burdens in the afterlife. Today, these offerings also take the shape of other items of monetary value, including bank notes, luxury clothes and even smartphones. The Hungry Ghost Festival is a time for reverent ancestral worship, a reminder of our ongoing duties to honour the departed.

5
DEVILISH DRINKS

Brew up these hauntingly good drinks for a taste of something wicked. From the classic Dark 'n' Stormy, page 143, to an elusive, creamy concoction that summons the energy of the full moon, these nightcaps or afternoon tipples will keep any guest well and truly satiated.

Some of these recipes call for a cocktail shaker, but if you don't have one to hand, no problem! You can make do using a mason jar, large empty jam jar, protein shaker bottle, leakproof Tupperware or any other food container, as long as it comes with a lid! Just fill with your cocktail ingredients and ice, fasten the lid on tightly, and shake vigorously for as long as the recipe calls for.

✱ BLOOD ORANGE MARGARITA ✱

This cocktail blends vibrant, citrusy sweetness with a kick of something stronger. The beautiful blood oranges lend their bold colour and seasonal flavour to a classic margarita. With just the right amount of tartness, this blend has a certain bite to it that transforms the classic cocktail into something vampiric. Decorated with sprigs of rosemary and glistening slices of blood orange, these are utterly seductive.

Yield — 4 servings
Time — 10 minutes

Ingredients

- Sea salt
- 1 lime wedge
- Ice
- 300ml blood orange juice, about 4–5 blood oranges
- 180ml tequila
- 100ml fresh lime juice, about 3 medium limes
- 80ml Cointreau or any triple sec
- 2 tbsp honey (optional)
- sprigs of rosemary
- 4 blood orange slices

Method

1. Sprinkle a few teaspoons of sea salt over a small plate or inside a wide bowl. Next, rub a cut wedge of lime along the rim of four margarita glasses and then dip each into the sea salt so that the entire rim is covered. Set aside.
2. Fill a cocktail shaker with ice before adding the blood orange juice, tequila, lime juice, triple sec and honey, if using. Shake vigorously for 15–20 seconds.

3. Pour the mix into the prepared glasses over fresh ice. Serve each cocktail with a sprig of rosemary and blood orange slice.

✱ DARK 'N' STORMY ✱

Indulge in this deliciously mysterious cocktail, ready in just five minutes. The rich black rum brings notes of butterscotch and sweet spices, which are uplifted by the effervescent, punchy ginger beer and zesty fresh lime juice – a perfect storm of flavours. Refreshing, sweet and addictively spicy.

Yield — 4 servings
Time — 5 minutes

Ingredients

- 400ml ginger beer, chilled
- 80ml fresh lime juice, about 2–3 medium limes
- 200ml black rum, ideally Goslings Black Seal Rum
- 4 lime wedges

Method

1. Pour the ginger beer into four Collins or highball glasses over lots of ice. Next, add the lime juice and black rum. Don't stir to keep that stormy effect.
2. Garnish each drink with a wedge of lime.

✱ GIN & TONIC WITH BLACKBERRY BRAINS ✱

Jammy stewed blackberries bring some spook to this sophisticated cocktail. The tart sweetness of purple-black blackberry syrup combines with the botanical notes of gin and refreshing fizz of tonic water, making each glass both eye-catching and ghoulishly good.

Yield — 4 servings
Time — 25 minutes

Ingredients

- 300g blackberries
- 50g sugar
- 4 tbsp lime juice
- Ice
- 200ml gin
- 800ml tonic water
- 4 toothpicks

Method

1. Set aside eight whole blackberries and put the rest in a saucepan with the sugar. Stir to coat each berry and then cook on medium heat for about 10 minutes until they start to break down and get syrupy, stirring occasionally. Set aside to cool for about 10 minutes.
2. Fill four highball glasses with ice, add 50ml gin and 1 tbsp lime juice in each. Top off each with tonic water.
3. Finally, scoop equal measures of the cooled blackberry mixture into each glass, stirring gently.
4. To garnish, skewer two blackberries onto a toothpick and add one atop each drink.

✱ POISON APPLE CIDER ✱

As this bubbles away on the stove, your kitchen is going to smell like magic – tangy cider, sweet apples and warming cinnamon. A few glugs of dark rum give this autumnal blend some added complexity, while something mischievous lurks within... just a hint of fiery cayenne pepper. Make this recipe alcohol-free by substituting the cider with more apple juice and omitting the dark rum and dark brown sugar.

Yield — 6 to 8 servings
Time — 30 minutes

Ingredients

- 1 litre dry cider
- 80ml dark rum
- 300ml apple juice
- 75g dark brown sugar
- 1 orange, zest and juice
- 5 whole cloves
- 3 cinnamon sticks
- ½ tbsp allspice berries
- ⅛ tsp cayenne pepper

Method

1. Pour the cider, dark rum, apple juice and dark brown sugar into a large saucepan and gently heat until the sugar has dissolved.
2. Add the orange zest and spices before bringing to a simmer, keeping on a low heat for about 20–30 mins.
3. Once finished, ladle into mugs to serve.

✱ THE FULL MOON ELIXIR ✱

Smooth, creamy and a little wild. This drink is charged with the energy of the full moon, and anything is possible. Hints of vanilla from the effervescent cream soda are balanced with rich coconut milk. For mystical gatherings or quiet moments under the stars.

Yield — 4 to 6 servings
Time — 5 minutes

Ingredients

- 1 x 400ml can full-fat coconut milk
- 1 litre cream soda
- Ice

Method

1. In a large mixing jug, combine the coconut milk and cream soda. Stir until combined.
2. Divide the elixir into four to six glasses with ice. If you can get your hands on a circular ice maker, that would be the perfect addition – an icy moon in each glass.

The Moon, Mother of Monsters

The full moon, round and radiant, has long held a significant reputation in folklore as a mysterious force that summons feral transformations, intimately linked to supernatural activity. In many cultures, there are mythical creatures that share a kinship with the moon, the most prominent being the werewolf. Believed to be humans cursed (or gifted) with the ability to metamorphosise into a fearsome wolf under a full moon, these lupine man-beasts are well acquainted with the lunar cycles.

One of the earliest examples of werewolf legends is in Greek mythology, which tells the story of Lycaon, a king turned into a wolf by the god Zeus as a form of punishment for impiety. The term 'lycanthropy', which refers to the transformation of human beings into wolves, comes from this tale. In European medieval folklore, the werewolf was mostly associated with witchcraft and a divine punishment enacted by God. They were feared creatures known to be violent and bloodthirsty.

Their connection with the full moon was not a common element of lore during this time, however, but was popularised later in nineteenth-century literature and early cinema, which bound the werewolf's transformation to a symbolic lunar power. Throughout human history, cultures have told stories about the eerie and mysterious vision of the moon, sublime when it is at its fullest. It is no wonder that it eventually became so intertwined with the werewolf legend.

SPOOKY SNACKS

✱ ROASTED BUTTERNUT SQUASH DIP ✱

Made with sweet butternut squash, seasonal aromatics and tangy yoghurt, this savoury dip is perfect paired with warm pita, crackers or sliced vegetables. It's topped with pumpkin seeds, coriander and a drizzle of olive oil to balance warm autumnal flavours with a touch of freshness.

Yield — 4 servings
Time — 1 hour

Ingredients

- 400g butternut squash, diced
- 1 tbsp olive oil
- ½ tsp ground paprika
- ½ tsp ground cinnamon
- 1 onion, diced
- 2 garlic cloves, minced
- 2 tbsp plain yoghurt
- Sea salt and cracked black pepper, to taste

Toppings

- Pinch of ground paprika
- Fresh coriander, roughly chopped
- Pumpkin seeds
- Olive oil

Accompaniments

- Warm bread or pita
- Crackers
- Sea salt crisps
- Bell pepper or carrot batons
- Celery sticks

Method

1. Preheat the oven to 180°C/350°F and prepare a baking tray with greaseproof paper.
2. Peel and cut the butternut squash into about half-inch sized cubes before tossing in a large bowl with olive oil, sea salt, black pepper, paprika and cinnamon.
3. Place on the baking tray and roast in the oven for 30–40 minutes, or until tender and slightly caramelised.
4. While the butternut squash is in the oven, sauté the onion and garlic in a frying pan for 10 minutes until translucent. Set aside to cool.
5. Once the butternut squash is done, leave to cool for about 15 minutes. Next, place in a food processor with the yoghurt, onions and garlic. Blitz until smooth or leave a little chunky if you'd like. Taste for seasoning and make any adjustments.
6. Transfer to a bowl and top with a dusting of paprika, pumpkin seeds, fresh coriander and a drizzle of olive oil. Serve with your choice of accompaniment.

✱ CAPRESE EYEBALLS ✱

A spooky twist on the classic Italian Caprese salad. On a bed of fresh basil, cherry tomatoes, creamy mozzarella pearls and sliced black olives are layered to create the illusion of creepy eyeballs on a platter. The olive oil and balsamic dressing gives a sweetly acidic edge to this fresh salad. These Caprese eyeballs are frightfully simple to make and provide a lighter accompaniment to any rich treats on offer.

Yield — 20 eyeballs
Time — 20 minutes

Ingredients

- Fresh basil leaves
- 1 tbsp olive oil
- ¼ tbsp balsamic vinegar
- 10 cherry tomatoes
- Approx. 4 black olives
- 20 mozzarella pearls
- Sea salt and cracked black pepper, to taste

Method

1. Place the basil leaves on a serving plate and dress with olive oil, balsamic vinegar, salt and pepper.
2. Slice the cherry tomatoes in half lengthways and arrange on the basil leaves.
3. Chop the black olives widthways to make thin slices. Set aside.
4. On a chopping board, gently press each mozzarella pearl with the back of a spoon to flatten the round shape a bit.
5. Now layer up each eyeball with a mozzarella pearl base and piece of black olive as the pupil.
6. Keep in the fridge until ready to serve. Provide toothpicks or forks for guests.

✱ BLOODY POPCORN ✱

Freshly popped kernels of corn are covered in white chocolate with blood-red pops of freeze-dried raspberries. The burst of tart sweetness from the berries contrasts divinely with the rich, creamy white chocolate – rounded off with the satisfying crunch of the popcorn. Perfect for offering to guests on scary movie nights.

Yield — 2 to 4 servings
Time — 1 hour

Ingredients

- 100g popcorn kernels
- 150g white chocolate
- 1 tbsp freeze-dried raspberries pieces

Method

1. Prepare a baking tray lined with greaseproof paper.
2. If using microwave popcorn, prepare according to the package instructions. For regular popcorn kernels, heat 1–2 tablespoons of vegetable oil in a large pan. Add the kernels and stir to coat them in the oil. Place a lid on the pan and wait about five minutes or until the kernels stop popping. Every minute or so, give the pan a good shake. Lay the popcorn out on the lined baking tray and set aside to cool slightly.
3. Melt the white chocolate gently over a bain-marie or in the microwave at 30-second intervals, stirring often. Once melted, take off the heat and then mix in the freeze-dried raspberry pieces.

4. Drizzle the raspberry white chocolate over the popcorn and then place in the fridge for about 30 minutes until set. When ready to serve, break apart any clusters and transfer to a large bowl.

✱ CARAMEL APPLE SLICES ✱

There is something so magical about biting into a caramel apple. Perhaps because it recalls that childlike whimsy that feels synonymous with Halloween. These bite-sized versions will satisfy your craving for something sweetly nostalgic. The crisp green apple, buttery caramel, crunchy pecans and touch of sea salt make each mouthful the very essence of the season.

Yield — 4 to 6 servings
Time — 1 hour

Ingredients

- 15g pecans, finely chopped
- 60g golden caster sugar
- 1 tbsp water
- 30ml double cream
- 15g unsalted butter
- 3 green apples
- Sea salt

Method

1. Finely chop the pecans and set to one side.
2. Add the sugar to a pan on the stove with the water, cooking on medium heat until the sugar has dissolved.

3. Turn up to medium-high heat and bubble for 4–5 minutes until the caramel thickens, becomes a deep golden colour and gives off a slightly nutty aroma.
4. Take off the heat and then carefully stir in the double cream and unsalted butter. Set aside to cool for 15 minutes.
5. To stop your apple slices browning, slice them into wedges and then place them in a large bowl filled with 500ml of water and 1 teaspoon of dissolved sea salt. Soak the apple slices for 10 minutes and then drain, rinse and dry off. Arrange these slices on a serving platter.
6. Stir the cooled caramel and then drizzle it over the apple slices. Next, sprinkle on some chopped pecans and a pinch of sea salt, making sure each slice gets some.
7. Serve immediately with toothpicks or dessert forks.

Apple Bobbing

While caramel apples are a more recent invention (from fifties America), another holiday tradition that makes use of the popular fruit has a considerably older history. By the first century CE, the Roman Empire had conquered the majority of the Celtic lands, bringing about an intermingling of new customs and gods.

This includes the Roman festivals of Feralia and Pomona. The first is observed in late October to honour the passing of the dead. The latter is in celebration of the Roman goddess of orchard trees, Pomona, a wood nymph that represents fruitful abundance, her symbol an apple. Apple bobbing has roots in both this Roman celebration and Celtic Samhain traditions.

LOOKING THE PART

EASY AS (PUMPKIN) PIE HALLOWEEN COSTUMES

Leave the utter panic to horror movie characters. With a bit of creativity, and a rummage around in the back of your wardrobe, you can scrounge up the perfect Halloween look in no time at all (and likely without any extra spending). This is the no-stress approach to Halloween costumes, without losing any of the whimsy! These five ideas are easy, fun and charming. Perfect for any last-minute party invites.

1. **Witch**

To embody the witch, gather up all your black clothing – a long dress or flowing skirt paired with a blouse would be ideal. If you're averse to the colour black, a deep purple, green or blue will also work! Layer on shawls, capes, cardigans, necklaces or any interesting textures (lace, wool, metal, crystal, feathers, ribbon) you own to bring the witchy look to life. For makeup, apply black or dark tones to your eyelids and blend out for a sultry smoke. Pair with a dark lipstick and a swipe of mascara.

Optional

- Black hat (the pointier the better)
- Old wooden broomstick
- Wand
- Dusty leather spellbook
- Bundle of herbs

The Witch's Hat

For centuries, legends of mysterious women with mystical powers have endured in history and myth. Their practices are mostly rooted in pagan traditions and often linked to herbalism and spiritual healing – guardians of nature's wisdom. With the arrival of Christianity in medieval Europe, a rising fear of their assumed consort with darkness led to widespread witch hunts.

While the iconic long pointed black hat emerged in early modern Europe, it shares a lineage with popular fashions throughout the centuries, religious persecution of Jewish communities – who were made to wear distinguishing headwear – and was finally popularised in the seventeenth and eighteenth centuries through children's literature. From the thirties, the image of the witch was commercialised as a popular Halloween costume, also inspired by cultural touchstones such as *The Wizard of Oz*.

---

2. Wednesday Addams

A beloved character who shares our penchant for the morose. This costume is instantly recognisable and very easy to DIY. You'll need a white shirt or blouse with a large and structured collar to layer underneath a black, long-sleeved, knee-length dress. Opt for black tights or knee-high white socks and wear any sturdy black shoe (though Mary Janes or loafers would work best). Your makeup can be minimal, perhaps some eyeliner or mascara to darken your eyes. Keep the lips neutral – Wednesday wouldn't be caught dead in any shade of pink. Your hair needs to be parted down the middle and braided neatly into two side plaits. The last step is practising your deadpan delivery and brooding expression. Wow, you've got it already!

3. Zombie

Originating in Haitian folklore, in which they were believed to be reanimated corpses controlled by voodoo, the modern depiction of zombies is far more concerned with their unusual appetite. Popularised in horror movies throughout the latter half of the twentieth century, the zombie came to symbolise fears of spreading disease, societal collapse and loss of bodily autonomy.

Still have a taste for brains? Dig out those old worn clothes that you won't mind ripping up. Any outfit will work: jeans, suits or dresses. Armed with a pair of scissors, create tears and rips in several areas of the clothing. Use dustings of black or brown powder makeup (even instant coffee or cocoa will work), to create a more aged look. Then smear some fake blood or red lipstick on certain spots, making sure to dab more around your mouth. Use baby powder to give your face a lifeless sheen. Red, purple and green makeup can be rubbed into your skin to create the impression of bruises (or decaying flesh). Leave your hair undone – the messier the better.

4. Chucky

Did you know that Chucky's full name is Charles Lee Ray? It's a mash-up of some notorious serial killers – Charles Manson, Lee Harvey Oswald and James Earl Ray.

There is nothing more terrifying than a doll coming to life – talk about uncanny. If you plan on being a little bit mischievous this spooky season, Chucky is the perfect costume. Do you own a classic pair of denim overalls and a long-sleeved striped shirt (bonus points if it's red, blue or green)? Then you were destined to cosplay this tiny terror. If you aren't blessed with his signature ginger locks, you could buy some temporary colour hairspray. Pop on some red shoes and you're good to go.

Optional

- Toy knife
- Dishevelled red wig

5. Black Cat

A shadowy black cat is the height of elegance. You need another all-black outfit, but this time search for form-fitting clothing: jumpsuits or leggings are a great choice. Velvet or faux fur will add more of a cat-like quality. To make some ears, hot-glue felt or card triangles onto a black headband. You can also DIY a tail by pinning a length of ribbon or faux fur to the back of your waistband. Using black eyeliner or face paint, draw an upside-down triangle on the tip of your nose and three sets of whiskers on either side.

Optional

- Black paw gloves
- Black choker or collar necklace

The Mystical Tales of Black Cats

Superstitions have surrounded the humble black cat for centuries. These inky felines, like shadows in the night, have inspired both fear and favour across cultures and throughout time. They were held in profound reverence by the ancient Egyptians, but considered a bad omen in medieval European folklore. Their spooky significance has survived into the present day, with black cats now a fixture of Halloween celebrations and symbolism.

Admiration for cats can be traced back to ancient Egypt, with the black variety regarded as sacred beings. The goddess Bastet, deity of the home, fertility and protection, was depicted in old texts and art as a female figure with the head of a lioness or cat. Bastet's close association with domestic cats ensured that they were respected, and even worshipped, in Egyptian society. In fact, killing a cat – even by accident – was punishable by death! Black cats were often kept in the home to ward off evil spirits, providing divine protection for their owners.

Ancient Romans also honoured black cats, and they were known to accompany soldiers on the battlefield during their many conquests throughout Europe. As Christianity spread across the continent, pagan associations with animals were viewed with increasing suspicion. Thus began a shift for the black cat – from adored to feared. During the Middle Ages, they also became entangled in the rising hysteria around witchcraft and the supernatural. The nocturnal habits of cats further encouraged the change in reputation from heralds of good fortune to symbols of the unknown, and therefore evil.

In some parts of Europe, they were even burned alongside women accused of being witches.

In contrast to much of continental Europe, black cats were viewed more positively in England and Scotland. In English folklore, black cats were often considered good luck charms. Sailors were known to keep them on ships, believing they would ensure safe passage and favourable weather during their voyages. In Japan, black cats have also long been viewed as symbols of good luck and protection. The Maneki-neko, or 'beckoning cat', is a common talisman in Japanese culture. While the traditional Maneki-neko is white, black varieties are popular and believed to ward off maleficent spirits and misfortune.

Today, the black cat retains its close links with witchcraft and Halloween (we all know and love Salem from *Sabrina the Teenage Witch*), and festive decorations in the creature's likeness are popular. Despite our cultural shift away from superstitions, black cats are still less likely to be adopted at shelters – perhaps a result of these lingering beliefs. And so, if chosen, wear your black cat costume with pride! Let us honour all our feline friends this season, but especially the black cat.

Part 04

EVERLASTING SPOOKY SEASON

Like an incantation, spooky season can be brought back from the dead any time of year. This chapter shows you how to weave the mystical threads of the season into your everyday life, so that the spirit of Halloween becomes a living part of you each day of the year. From style inspiration to more rituals and otherworldly folktales, discover how to embrace the beauty of all things eerie, eternally.

10 WAYS TO KEEP THE SPIRIT OF HALLOWEEN ALIVE ALL YEAR ROUND

While Halloween festivities are usually bound to the month of October, with a few tricks up your sleeve, you can relive these seasonal delights whenever you desire. Whether scorching in the summer heat or hibernating in the thick of winter, the magical hum of the holiday can be revived.

1. Transform Your Abode

Turn your living space into the evocation of a grand gothic home owned by a vampire residing in the misty mountains of Transylvania. By drawing inspiration from this romantically morbid style, you can surround yourself with its otherworldly allure from dusk to dawn. Here are some design tips to achieve this:

1. Build a colour palette of the deepest blacks, dusty greys, deep purples and emerald greens.

2. Seek out dark wood furniture at the antiques shop. While you're there, look for ornate candlesticks, candelabras and vintage mirrors.
3. For your very own cabinet of curiosities, collect skull ornaments, old apothecary bottles and any other terrifying trinkets you happen upon.
4. Choose velvet, lace and satin fabrics.
5. Enhance the mood by burning woody incense or essential oils like patchouli, clove and cedarwood to create a mysterious and earthy aroma.

2. Dress for the Occasion

If your home now looks like a charmingly haunted house, why not also dress the part? When crafting your mood board, search for gothic, Victorian and whimsigoth styles to find what feels right for you – from sorceress of the dark to a dreamy cottage witch. Start small with some bat wing earrings or a delicate skull necklace. Build your colour palette around black (of course) and deep purples, blues, reds and greys. Indulge in velvet, lace, tulle, leather and silk to create an elegant yet edgy look. Make sure you layer up on crystal pendants, silver jewellery and plenty of celestial accessories. My advice? A dark lip will bring together any outfit with a touch of brooding magic.

3. Host Clandestine Gatherings

Invite your friends and family over for a scary movie marathon, intimate tarot reading or mystical late-night feast. Whatever time of year, set the scene with twinkling candles, fairy lights, vintage lace tablecloths and dark seasonal florals or dried flowers. You can revive the spooky spirit of autumn with a playlist of folksy, gothic tunes while you reconnect with loved ones over a witches' brew of choice. Bring your circle of friends together to drink wine and share secrets – don't forget to offer tantalising snacks such as dark chocolate with sea salt, spiced nuts and a platter of seasonal fruits.

4. Be Transported by Art

Nothing beats that feeling of escaping into a spooky novel or getting lost in the haunting beauty of a gothic horror flick. Return to our reading and watch lists for an extensive library of ghostly media to ignite that Halloween vibe anytime, anywhere. You could even delve into the poetry of Edgar Allan Poe, whose dark, yearning, melancholic verse perfectly captures the spirit of the season, or visit your local art museum showing a collection of Victorian Gothic art. Get swept up in painting, literature, poetry and cinema – portals straight to October.

5. Keep a Witchy Journal

Wield your pen like a wand as you cast spells in your journal for introspection and blossoming. Use your journal as a sacred space by recording daily musings, writing gratitude lists, re-evaluating goals or even writing letters to your future self. Sustain autumn's lessons of renewal by letting your emotions flow. This is an empowering practice that helps you tap into your inner witchy wisdom and honour the transformative energy of autumn in each and every season.

6. Surround Yourself with Fall Scents

From skincare to candles, you can infuse the warm and smoky spice of autumn into your space, capturing the earthy richness of the season. Whether you crave cosy moments or desire a more brooding scent, curate the aromas that cling to your skin or gently cloak your home. Think cinnamon scrubs and ambery perfumes. Here are some more seasonal scents to seek out:

- Pumpkin spice and chai blends with cinnamon, nutmeg, clove and a hint of vanilla
- Apple cider, orange peel and tart cranberries
- Sticky maple syrup and brown sugar
- Smoky or woody perfumes

7. Take Strolls Through Cemeteries

Even without the crackling leaves and crisp autumn air, cemeteries have a serene and reverent beauty that can provide a connection to the past and a gentle reminder of the sanctity of existence. Taking a quiet stroll through these hallowed grounds is another way to honour the spirit of Halloween, one that asks us to show respect to those who have passed, but also embrace the natural cycle of life and death.

8. Celebrate Each & Every Full Moon

Beyond the Harvest Moon that takes place in October, every lunar cycle holds profound meaning throughout the year. Celebrating each full moon is a wonderful way to connect with the rhythms of the natural world and move freely with the changing seasons. Study the moon's influence on your personal birth chart to nurture deeper understanding about how it affects you directly. Set aside time each month to journal your intentions and release what no longer serves you. Practise grounding exercises such as meditation or yoga to bring clarity to your desires. You can also take a calming bath infused with herbal salts, make some moon water or take a peaceful walk under the glowing moonlight.

9. Bake Spooky Sweet Treats No Matter the Season

Like brewing potions, return to the art of baking something spooky year-round to satisfy your sweet tooth. With a handy can of pumpkin purée, you can make a tender pumpkin bread or pumpkin pie brownies whatever the season. Or perhaps bake another batch of almond cookies, shaped like witches' fingers, to bring some magic back into your kitchen. With a pinch of cinnamon and a dash of whimsy, you can taste the autumn air, with a sugary kiss, whenever you please.

10. Stay Mischievous

Though Halloween is a time for reverence, as well as tales of grotesque creatures and ghosts gone awry, there is an innocent kind of joy in letting your imagination run wild during the holiday. Carry this feeling with you beyond 31 October and embrace the mischievousness of the season – tell a ghost story to a new friend, don a witch's hat in the middle of spring or take an unexpected trip to an enchanted forest. If you bring some magic and mystery to the mundane, the spirit of Halloween will never die.

✱ WHAT ELSE LURKS ✱ IN THE SHADOWS...

In every culture on earth, unearthly creatures have haunted our imaginations and shaped the folklore tales that we share by firelight. These strange, elusive beings blur the boundaries between the natural and supernatural, serving as cautionary tales that remind us to respect the immense power of nature, for there is much we don't know about this world.

While fearsome monsters such as vampires, zombies and werewolves are more commonly associated with Halloween, helped by their popularity in modern media, here are some other legends told around the world that might capture your imagination. By now, you know to keep your wits about you during Halloween, when spirits freely roam, but by paying respect to the preternatural any time of year, you evoke the holiday's reverence for the unexplainable and help keep these rich stories alive.

Whatever the season, but especially when the early hours seem just a touch too quiet, ponder what might be watching you from the dark – and remember the lessons they bring.

The Lightning Bird - South Africa

The Lightning Bird, or Impundulu, is a large vampiric bird from the folklore of the Zulu people. This black-and-white bird is about the size of a person and is believed to use its wings or sharp talons to summon storms, thunder and lightning.

With a ravenous thirst for blood, it is known to take the form of an attractive young man to seduce its female prey. Often the familiar of a witch, the Impundulu is also closely linked to witchcraft. This immortal being is difficult to kill, passed down through the many generations of the witches it serves. The Lightning Bird embodies the wild, untameable forces of nature: both divine and destructive. Like the witches it accompanies, it reminds us to respect nature's duality as an essential balance.

Black Annis - England

A fearsome figure in English folklore, Black Annis is a hag or witch said to have eerie blue skin and claw-like hands, used to snatch children straight from their homes or more likely if they've wandered too far from safety. She will then devour her innocent victims and hang their skins in the dark forest cave where she resides. Some say that Black Annis was once a woman rejected by society or grieving the loss of her family. Others suggest she is an ancient spirit of nature twisted by time into a malevolent being. No doubt an effective reminder for children to not go venturing out after dark.

Vodyanoy - Russia
This water spirit from Slavic mythology is depicted as an elderly man with a bloated, amphibian body, and can have a greenish beard, webbed fingers or slimy algae in his hair. Both feared and revered, the Vodyanoy lives in whirlpools within lakes, rivers and ponds, where it is believed he drags unsuspecting victims, or especially those who pollute the water, into the depths to drown. Because he rules over all watery domains, millers were thought to have a special relationship with him in order to avoid accidents, bringing offerings to the riverbank to appease him.

* A POCKET GUIDE TO SUMMERWEEN *

The term 'Summerween' originates from a 2012 episode of the animated TV show, *Gravity Falls*, in which the residents of the titular town celebrate Halloween twice a year, the second time being on 22 June. During these summertime festivities, watermelons are used to carve jack-o'-melons and people tell tales of the Summerween Trickster – a monster that eats children who don't respect the spirit of the holiday.

This little guide is brief but will help you celebrate the joy that is Summerween – and appease the Trickster – so that spooky season can have its chance to bask in the sun as well.

Watermelon Carving
There is nothing more refreshing than a sweet slice of watermelon on a hot day. While you carve your spooky design,

snack on those fruity chunks to stay happy and hydrated. Blitz any leftovers into a summer smoothie or pop into a fruit salad. You'll find that a melon is a bit easier to cut into than a pumpkin, and makes a surprisingly fearsome face. Delicious and devilish.

Honouring the Summer Solstice

Just as Halloween shares cultural traditions with the harvest season and autumn equinox, Summerween is the perfect time to observe the summer solstice and connected folklore celebrations.

The summer solstice, occurring around 20–21 June in the Northern Hemisphere, is the longest day of the year. Ancient cultures such as the Celts and Druids commemorated this event with bonfires and bountiful feasts. Like Halloween, it is also believed that the veil between physical and spiritual worlds is thin at this time – what a beautiful seasonal mirror! Midsommar, celebrated in Scandinavia, marks the longest day of the year as well as the strength of the sun, nature's abundance and fertility.

* SOME WAYS TO JOIN IN THE FESTIVITIES *

Make a Flower Crown

An ancient symbol of divinity and rebirth, flower crowns are worn during the summer solstice to ward off evil spirits and honour the season. Weaving summer's flora into a crown, for yourself or another, connects you to the season. Find a circular ring or natural wood crown that fits comfortably to use as a base or simply weave each flower into the next using their stems – like a daisy chain. Marigolds, daisies, peonies and wildflowers are just some of the flowers in bloom. It is also believed that flowers and herbs foraged during this day have magical properties. As you weave your lush and fragrant crown, set intentions for growth and renewal.

Watch the Sunrise & Sunset

Mark the longest day of the year by rising early to catch the sunrise and then later watching the sunset. Find a quiet spot in nature to ground yourself to the earth's rhythms. Sit atop a grassy hill or nestled on a picnic blanket in your back garden. Wherever you choose, focus on the warmth of the sun on your skin as it blinks in and out of the horizon. Bring a journal to gather your thoughts, set intentions or simply express gratitude for the light of the season. Take pleasure in your own company or share each moment with friends – you decide how to honour the daylight.

Light a Bonfire

Bonfires are common in rituals from Norse to Baltic traditions, where they are usually lit on midsummer's eve to celebrate the sun's radiant strength as it sits at the highest point in the sky, and to bring about other benefits, like warding off evil spirits and ensuring a fruitful upcoming harvest. Using a firepit or campfire, invite your loved ones along to take part in a purifying bonfire. Each take turns writing something you hope to let go of on a piece of paper, and then toss it into the fire!

✱ A SUMMERWEEN ✱ WATCHLIST

Though scary movies are often shrouded in thick fog or darkness, this selection is just as exhilarating. Though the sun's warm glow usually inspires optimistic feelings, the harsh light of day also means there's nowhere to hide. From surreal folk horror to campy summer blockbusters, these films are spooky with an added heat.

Friday the 13th (1980, Sean S. Cunningham)

This is a summer camp slasher classic! Young counsellors at Camp Crystal Lake are being picked off one by one by a ruthless killer. Blood-soaked and suspenseful, with one hell of a twist, *Friday the 13th* defined eighties horror. This film also kicked off one of horror's most infamous franchises.

Midsommar (2019, Ari Aster)

A horror film that takes place almost entirely in broad daylight, *Midsommar* is disturbingly beautiful. It follows Dani, a grieving young woman who travels with her friends to a Swedish community to celebrate the Midsummer festival, which descends into ritualistic terror. This movie is sun-soaked madness.

The Lost Boys (1987, Joel Schumacher)

Welcome to Santa Carla – murder capital of the world. This California beach town is home to a gang of teenage vampires sporting leather jackets and riding around on motorcycles. *The Lost Boys* is stylish, camp and gory, a cult classic worth seeing while the sun is blazing.

Jaws (1975, Steven Spielberg)

This classic was the first summer blockbuster, and managed to traumatise a whole generation. In *Jaws*, a great white shark terrorises a coastal town in New England, stirring up heart-shredding suspense as you wait for the predator to strike again. With an unforgettable score and special effects that still hold up to this day, watching Spielberg's masterpiece is a no-brainer.

Scooby-Doo (2002, Raja Gosnell)

The gang's all here! When Daphne, Fred, Scooby-Doo, Shaggy and Velma reunite at Spooky Island, a vacation resort, they must unravel yet another mystery as guests start disappearing under mysterious circumstances. This campy live-action film of the beloved animated TV show is silly, nostalgic and spooky without the screams.

* A CLOSING CHARM *

Thank you, kindred spirit, for walking the shadowy path of all things spooky with me. Together, we have journeyed into the past, whispered spells of gratitude and discovered the spellbinding work of sugary treats. As the nights grow longer with encroaching autumn, may your days be touched with magic and mischief – and as you know by now, the magic of the season never truly ends. You can find it in each flicker of a candle, some dancing steam rising from a pot of herbal tea, or hidden within the pages of that gloomy Gothic novel.

Stay wild, curious and eternally spooky.

✱ INDEX ✱